D1360686

ABANDONED AND SHATTERED

Surviving and Thriving After the
Pain of a Breakup You Didn't Want

Copyright © 2017 Daryl A. Moore

All rights reserved. No part of this book may be used or reproduced in any manner without written permission from the author and publisher.

This work is intended only for personal growth and related education. It should not be treated as a substitute for professional assistance, mental health activities such as psychotherapy or counseling, or any form of medical advice. In the event of physical or mental distress, please contact appropriate professionals. The application and activities resulting from the information in this book is the choice of each reader, who assumes full responsibility for his or her understandings, interpretations, and results. The author and publisher assume no responsibilities for the actions or choices of any reader.

Published 2017

Book formatting and cover design by István Szabó, Ifj.

Author photos by Leo Peterson

Printed by CreateSpace, An Amazon.com Company

Printed in the United States of America library of Congress cataloguing-in-publication data

13 9 7 8 1 9 7 6 3 2 8 4 3 5

Moore, Daryl 2017

Abandoned and shattered: surviving and thriving after the pain of a breakup you didn't want

Tradepaper ISBN: 978-1976328435

ABANDONED AND SHATTERED

Surviving and Thriving After the Pain of a Breakup You Didn't Want

DARYL MOORE

For my children, Deidre, Dylan, and Devon Moore. You each inspire me to focus on my purpose and remind me of what is truly important in life. I love you very much.

To my readers, without your trust in me and allowing me to support you through my ideas, my work would be for nothing. I have been where you are today and I know what is possible. Thank you!

"Persistence and resilience only come from having been given the chance to work through difficult problems."

— Gever Tulley

"Patience and perseverance have a magical effect before which difficulties disappear and obstacles vanish."

— John Quincy Adams

Contents

Acknowledgements

Writing this book was by no means only an individual effort. Committed people behind the scenes made this project possible. My deepest gratitude goes to the following individuals:

My son Devon, you have brought so much unconditional love and positive energy to my life. I am proud to be your dad. I am always here for you no matter how life is treating you. I love you Devon.

My daughter Deidre, thank you for keeping an open mind after the divorce. I enjoy our movie nights and discussions. You are age 23 now and it has been my greatest joy to see you grow as a person. You will always be my little girl. Love you.

My ex-wife, Desiree, for all of your mutual support since Dylan passed away in 2015. We have learned a lot of lessons together about co-parenting and handling loss since the divorce. We have had a seamless relationship with our other two children and I credit you for your partnership in their well-being. Thank you for being a friend.

My close friend Annette Provenza, you have been there night and day to support my vision, give honest feedback, and be present for me through both dark and light. Thank you for not letting me lower my standards even when times seemed challenging at best.

My father, Brain Moore, you have been my role model throughout my life. You lead by example and remind me to never quit and never lose sight of my values. You have supported me and added to my courage to go after big dreams. I love you dad.

My stepmother, Cheryl Moore, you taught me the value of respect and hard work, which have created a lasting impression. Our weekly conversations mean the world to me. I appreciate all that you stand for in life and respect that you always put your passion behind your values. You have all my love and respect.

My long-term and loving friend, Anita Lopez-Cech. You were instrumental on my path toward a higher consciousness and helped me through some habits that were keeping me in a dark hole. You are pure love and inspiration. The journey of truth we share is truly amazing.

My energetic and loyal friend Lilliy Johnson, for helping with the formatting and graphic elements of the internal book design. You are a ray of light and your humor and wit make life tolerable.

My friend since childhood, Carol Semple, you have served as a passionate example of what it means to set up a vision and make it happen. You have rubbed off on me positively over the years.

My friend and advisor, Jawed Ahmad Nassiri, you were there since day one and have seen the best and worst of me. Thank you for always caring and getting me to see multiple views of the situation.

I have numerous mentors, relationships, and inspiring teachers along the way, both in person and through their works: Michele Weiner-Davis, Melissa Smith-Gosier, Leo Peterson, Brendon Burchard, Philippe Ray, Lucille Peterson, Mike Koenigs, Tony Robbins, Arnold Schwarzenneger, Gary Vaynerchuk, Tony Jeary, John Assaraf, Sandra Anne Taylor, Sara Bareilles, Dr. Wayne Dyer, Les Brown, Seth Godin, Jeff Taylor (JT), Tim Ferriss, Bonnie Zanetti, Michael Hyatt, Jayme Barrett, Oprah Winfrey, Steven Pressfield, Dr. Sanjay Jain, Dr. Bruce Lipton, Dr. Joe Dispenza, John C. Maxwell, Dr. Joe Vitale, Frank Kern, Jeff Walker, Marie Forleo, and Brian Tracy.

Preface

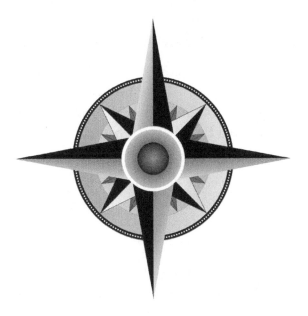

My Journey

"Resilience is accepting your new reality, even if it's less good than the one you had before. You can fight it, you can do nothing but scream about what you've lost, or you can accept that and try to put together something that's good."
— Elizabeth Edwards

The knock came at my front door. When I opened the door, two men were standing there with a large envelope. One of the gentlemen asked the dreaded question: "Are you Daryl Moore?" I responded with "yes" and they proceeded to have me sign for the packet he was holding. I remember my hands shaking as I saw the papers.

My heart was speeding up at an uncontrollable rate. I was sweating and numb at the same time. I had a mad rush of negative emotions going through my head. My world was falling apart. I knew the day of divorce was coming, but I wasn't sure when.

When I opened the packet, and saw the words Dissolution of Marriage at the top, my heart sunk. Divorce is the last thing I wanted. My mind went to the darkest of places faster than I ever thought it could.

I called my wife while she was at work and asked how she could do this. She apologized and said, "I planned for the papers to be served at home instead of a day you were working so I didn't embarrass you." I was shocked. This was a relationship that reached the better part of 30 years and I couldn't understand a reason in the world it could not be worked out. My dream of my relationship died at that time. I stood there crying and shaken like a truck had run over me.

After I experienced the initial emotions, the fears began to set in. How would this divorce negatively impact the kids? How would I get to be with my kids when the courts favored mothers? How could I afford to pay child support with tight finances and have to carry another place to live? Would it all fall apart? Would I need multiple roommates? Where would the kids sleep if I could get my share of the custody? How could I afford everything I needed for a new place? How would property be divided? Not only did I feel deeply abandoned, I felt an intense negative feeling that would follow me around for weeks.

My guess is that you have some similar thoughts to mine at this point. You probably have more questions than answers right now. I wrote this book for you because I know the suffering and deep pain that occurs when we don't feel wanted or needed any longer.

In my opinion, there are very few experiences in life more painful than a breakup we did not want, or did not expect. The pages to follow will take you on a journey past the pain and challenges and to a place where you can recover and redefine the future. I came out on the other side a transformed person and you can too.

Before getting started on this path together, I decided to share my painful yet transforming story with you so that you can see that you are not alone and that I am very human. Like anyone else, I have imperfections that have added stress where it was not needed. I have lived in pain that made life more difficult than it needed to be. The experience of highs and lows had been my existence, and will be shared with you in the pages to come.

It is my goal that this book and my story will illuminate a path for you that will lead to hope and certainty for your future. My wish is that this story clearly offers key exposures and lessons that led to some of my largest and most inspiring decisions in life. My deepest wish is that my story, and the resources in this book, will help you get back on your feet. I know it can't be easy for you now. I also know that huge changes are possible in a hurry with the right focuses, even if that seems out of reach at the moment.

Key Decisions

My parent's breakups and reconnections started back when we lived in Virginia and made their way to Colorado after we relocated. At the age of 13 my parents finally divorced. As children, we often do not understand why things happen the way they do. I remember consistent fighting going on between my parents. My mom and dad triggered the worst behaviors in each other and it was a living hell while it was going on. They were both good people, just not great together.

Nights existed where all I remember is screaming back and forth between my parents. I would not classify myself as having a happy childhood. There were magical moments I remember from my childhood, yet as kids we tend to generalize our childhood as either good or bad. I classified mine as negative due to a home that was not peaceful a percentage of the time.

At the time of my parent's divorce, I remember making the decision that if I was ever to marry, I would marry the right woman and stay married forever. This decision was based on the experience I had when my parents were fighting. The decision was also based on the mind of a child. Still, the commitment stuck with me until the divorce of my marriage in 2014. It is amazing how we choose values at such an early age that will guide the rest of our lives. The decision to find the right woman and stay married forever was a tall order for me to live up to.

Immediately following high school, I served in the United States Navy. I kept my values of waiting for the ideal relationship alive during my entire time in the military. I turned down numerous relationships due to the decision I made when my parents divorced. After getting out of the Navy I returned to Colorado.

Finding the Right Partner

I met who would become my wife when I was managing health and fitness facilities. She exercised consistently and this gave me the chance to see her often at one of the health clubs I managed. She tended to offset my outgoing and direct personality with a more reserved and family-driven focus. That was refreshing for me.

Her parents remained married through death. My parents were divorced, and I saw that as a liability on my end since I didn't have an example of how to make relationships work. My new girlfriend (who became my wife) was the ideal family person to guide me with the chaos of my own family at that time.

I had a hard time believing that a family gets together at least once a week or more. My own family felt obligated to get together for just holidays. I did make effort to form a bond with my parents and siblings outside of holidays, but it was nothing compared to the time my girlfriend spent with her family.

In addition to some very special qualities I saw in my girlfriend, the family centered element is what eventually made me commit to marriage. I was happy and had my ideal spouse for a lifetime!

During our long relationship, we raised three gorgeous kids together. I was scared beyond belief to have children with anyone. Somehow it felt natural having children with her. I was keeping my promise to stay married to one person forever. I was living up to the label I had created for myself as a teen. When life was aligned to how I thought it should be, times were euphoric.

When the Problems Started

There were a number of triggers that started to create problems in our relationship. I refuse to make either of us the bad person or the lopsided cause of the problems. In my humble opinion, it was a mutual deterioration over time that caused issues.

From my perception, I feel like I subconsciously took it for granted that she was such a great family person. I could work on a career in an unbalanced way and feel like I would not have a price to pay. I put her on a pedestal in terms of her family focus. I worked long hours, went to school and obtained a Bachelor's degree in psychology and two Master's Degrees. She took care of the family the majority of the time and kept things afloat at home.

With homework, long work hours, travel for the career, and a variety of additional obligations, the pressure of raising the kids mostly on her own was killing her internally. I loved the kids and wanted to be with them. I also felt the increasing obligation to be a supreme breadwinner and growing as much as possible in my career.

This lack of balance started creating issues and I did not even notice at the time that my relationship started to deteriorate. Our conversations became harsher, the attacks began, and her parents passing away just added to the stress. We also had a surprise child when we were age 40, and he has been nothing short of a miracle child. Even having our miracle baby, it added additional stress to the areas that already were not working.

The conversations almost always turned into some form of argument. It was predictable like the sunset how each topic of conversation would go. I would say one thing and she would respond in a conditioned manner. I would do the same until a vicious circle of communications became the outcome. After a while, accusations would start about who did what. Finally, when someone felt stabbed emotionally deep enough, one of us would flee the scene. The silence was often deafening.

I was not proud of the things I said. I felt like I was retaliating for the harsh things she said. The problems had been brewing for quite some time and we became so distant we were unsure how to build a bridge back. She is an extremely proud person as I am. I couldn't stop the fallout and we were both getting more damaged emotionally the longer we stayed together.

Finally, the communications completely broke down and she mentioned a divorce. I knew from the way she announced the divorce that it was only a matter of time until she filed. I moved down to our walkout basement and transformed my office into a bedroom. I purchased a queen-sized air bed to get me by until I could hopefully get her to see the light in our marriage. I eventually expanded to a king size bed in my office. I sat back and watched the marriage crumble.

The Start of the End

I remember already missing her even though we remained in the same house. We raised our kids jointly in that house. I did everything I could to try to get her to connect with me. I emailed long notes. I wrote letters. I called her. I tried to generate conversation whenever I could. The more I tried, the more she distanced. I felt like she hated me. I wasn't giving her room to breathe because I simply could not imagine a divorce and my family breaking up. I am not the type of person who just stops trying and retreats, but I was making it worse. Things were getting out of control.

The months that followed became horrible. I didn't want to miss time with my kids so I remained in the family home. We would sometimes have dinner on the main floor but a majority of time the main floor was like a ghost town. The kids would go upstairs to the master bedroom where my wife was staying, or into their own rooms. They would also come down to the walkout basement where I was staying. We rarely had family time on the middle floor.

After some grueling comments from fights, I began having alcohol to drown out the heavy hits emotionally. I didn't drink to blackout but with a couple of rum and cokes a night I could numb some of the pain. I remember asking myself which Netflix series I wanted to start next. I would turn on the TV, pour a drink, and begin to alter the reality I was living in. I found a comfortable space emotionally periodically and placed my life on hold while I waited for her to file a divorce.

Comments from friends and family were usually around the question of why I would not file for the divorce myself, so I could move on and be free of the negativity. The decision of a lifelong marriage that I made at 13 years old was haunting me now. I was in a world of hurt and felt I had no choice but to deal with it. When I made the decision to stay married until death, I did not account for the other 50 percent of the relationship wanting out.

The divorce papers finally arrived, which I described at the start of the preface. I confronted the fact that it was ending and started creating plans to live with the reality of upcoming life.

Losing Our Home to a House Fire

A turning point in the marriage came shortly after the divorce papers were served. While living under the same roof as my wife I could see more and more distractions coming into the picture. My daughter was age 17 and was struggling in the negative environment. She attracted a man who was nine years older than her. He was only in the relationship to use her and take all he could from us.

She ran away with him. After a short time, we received a phone call from our daughter advising us that they were homeless. We were happy to take our daughter back into our home but I was against letting her boyfriend move in. My wife was worried that if she didn't offer for him to stay with us, she felt our daughter would not return. Ultimately, I didn't want to create turmoil and agreed to let him stay with us if he obtained a job. He demolished the food in our fridge and was completely disrespectful. He did not help with the chores of the house and was a slob that added to the messes that us working people had to clean up.

Shortly after he moved in, I was enjoying an NFL playoff game in my space downstairs. Suddenly I heard the screams saying, "Fire! fire! fire! Get out of the house." After ensuring everyone was out of the house, I ran outside and noticed the fire was blazing on the south side of the home. It had reached about 10 feet in height and nothing we did extinguished or slowed down the rising flames.

The fire department arrived less than 10 minutes later but it was too late. The damage was done. Between water, smoke, and fire damage, we lost about 80 percent of the house. It turned out that my daughter's boyfriend put a cigarette out on the side of the home. The boyfriend did not own up to the fire being caused by him, but the truth came out later. We had to have the house rebuilt, we relocated to a hotel, then transitioned into a rental house until our home was finished.

My wife pulled the divorce off the table temporarily. Our marriage was no better than prior. Since we had insurance issues to deal with, living in a rental home while our house was demolished and rebuilt, and kids who were scared and displaced, the logical choice was to delay the divorce.

I dismissed the boyfriend permanently from the rental house after his friction with me and the family. Shortly after, we returned to our original home and when the re-construction was complete.

Some of the same negative relationship patterns continued in our re-built family home. My wife and I became a stronger team because of the work required from the house fire, but it was still not enough to pull the marriage back to a hopeful state.

My wife wanted to help her brother get through some challenges he was having, and allowed him and his girlfriend to move into our newly completed home. We went from one house guest to another. The latest guests were the straw that broke the camel's back. It shifted the dynamic of the household and again a divorce was announced and filed shortly after.

Luckily, because of the past divorce filing, I had created a contingency plan knowing divorce was probably coming again. The plan put me in a better position to handle the latest divorce announcement and filing. It was as if I had already been through a dress rehearsal.

Even with my contingency plan in hand, my heart dropped and my body was visibly shaken when the new papers were ready. Again, I started cycling through the range of emotions on a repetitive loop. I had fear of what was next, uncertainty, hopelessness, regret, unworthiness, rejection, blame, anger, frustration, and any other emotion that made me feel less than dirt. Like a CD that keeps playing, my conditioned behaviors had me right back trying to change her mind about the divorce. After seeing no receptivity on her part about reconciliation, I realized that this divorce was happening no matter what my wishes were. After all she was right. The marriage wasn't working.

My Final Attempt to Save My Marriage

My dad contacted me and advised me of specialist on last chance marriage-saving strategies named Michele Weiner-Davis. I picked up two books authored by her. The first was *Divorce Busting: A Step-By-Step Approach to Making Your Marriage Loving Again,* and the second newer book has the title, *The Divorce Remedy: The Proven 7-Step Program for Saving Your Marriage.* I wanted to go down fighting, so I vowed to master what Michele taught in the books.

The Divorce Remedy book could not have come at a better time for me. My marriage was technically dead, so any bit of advice could help at this point. The technique I started with is called, *The Last Resort*

Technique. This technique is used when extreme situations are taking place and divorce (or a breakup) seems inevitable.

The technique showed me all of the things I *shouldn't do* when my wife wanted out of the marriage. Michele said to stop telling my wife "I love you" because it was adding the increased pressure of guilt for her about leaving and knowing the marriage failed. Adding pressure wouldn't help me achieve my goal of keeping us together.

The Last Resort Technique had me doing a complete 180 of what I was currently doing that was not working. The first step in the process was to stop the chase (any efforts to pursue my wife). Michele described the advantages and importance of getting a life of my own and advised to return to doing things to make *my* life better. Though the technique may have had my wife wondering why suddenly I stopped pursuing her, she ultimately had made up her mind to divorce.

Michele's book was a monumental breakthrough for me because I was finally placing the focus on me again. I felt better because my mind wasn't on the failing marriage anymore. It was a win/win because the ultimate goal is to move on, with the marriage or without, but in a healthy way either way. Michele now has a video course on the *Last Resort Technique* and I highly recommend it if you legitimately think there is a relationship to save. See the resource section for the url to her online video course and for a listing of her books.

On a side note, I sent Michele an email to thank her for inspiring me to keep my sanity while going through my divorce. She had mentioned self-care as a needed ingredient to living life, which changed my focus. She has been gracious with her time. Michele is the expert on her topic. She repetitively appeared on Oprah and had tons of national television press because of her success in saving marriages and relationships. I wanted to include her here since it was a huge part of my recovery.

Once my wife filed the divorce, I had time to put life into perspective. My fear turned to anger and I advised my wife that no less than 50 percent of the time with the children was acceptable for me. Even though I was afraid of the perception of judges offering favoritism to the wife in the divorce, it was a must that I aimed to get equal time with my kids.

Luckily my wife was agreeable and also left me in a good arrangement financially. As I look back, we had an extremely amicable divorce compared to most others. No attorneys were utilized and we are on good terms to this day. There are occasional conflicts but they are never large and are easily resolved, and without involvement of the kids in the middle. We communicate consistently and our kids get to witness how mom and dad help each other.

Following the Divorce

After the divorce finalized in April of 2014, I contracted to have a new home built 30 minutes outside of town. Getting a new home outside of town helped me save money and allowed a fresh start and energy for me and the kids. I rented an apartment for the eight months the house was being built. After moving into the apartment, and on the weeks my kids weren't there, I experienced a deep loneliness and felt the negative emotions of the divorce again. I continued to drink rum and cokes to offset the pain, and neglected my diet. The severity was not as extreme as prior, but the habits still lingered.

I was committed to work, almost to a fault. I worked extreme hours during the weeks I didn't have the kids with me. I was not yet dealing with my divorce. I was just doing daily pump-ups to feel good emotionally for a brief time, but was not progressing. At that time, I resented my ex-wife for breaking up our family and was in the mindset that I would show her that she made a huge mistake. I no longer contacted her unless it was about the kids. I was mostly free of the negative energy from the relationship, but had to still deal with unresolved issues in myself. My quest was to improve myself and take the blame and anger off my ex-wife.

In the weeks before moving into my home, I suddenly started feeling inspired again. It had been a long time since I felt inspired. I picked up a book titled, "Feng Shui Your Life" by Jayme Barrett. This book started me on a good energy path for my home. I wanted this house to be a symbol of where I was heading instead of where I had been.

The book was so much more than just designing the rooms. Jayme outlined living a more successful life philosophically. This was a pivotal point in me moving forward. I realized that if I could just create a better consistent energy and outlook I could be in the position to make changes that would impact the future positively.

This was the first time since the start of the relationship problems that I felt like I owned my life again. Qualifying on my own home loan was fantastic since our past family home was a joint loan with my ex-wife. The new loan was a proclamation that I was in control of my life once again.

Having this freedom reminded me of an artist who had a blank canvass and could paint whatever picture they felt like painting, and I knew I could make it into a masterpiece. I felt a wave of warm water over me as I took actions in my positive new direction.

More Devastating News: The Death of Our Son

I was feeling good about life again and then on June 30, 2015, I received a call that would once again change my life. It was ex-wife screaming as she and my daughter came home and found our 14-year-old son had committed suicide. I was with our nine-year old son at the time and the call came across the Bluetooth in my car, allowing our younger son to hear everything. I made the dreadful drive across town to meet with the Coroners at my ex-wife's house.

During the drive, I was trying to answer our younger son's questions about Dylan dying without knowing myself the details of what had happened. After dropping off our younger son at a friend's while my ex-wife and I met with the Coroner, I could see that my life was completely out of control and I was angry and at a loss for words. I was at my ex-wife's house all evening as family came by to see us. This nightmare was continuing to grow.

After our son's death, many people were at a loss about what to say to us. People we considered good friends were suddenly non-existent any longer. People who we never thought would have a thing to do with us showed up with hugs and support, and many supplied stories of their own losses.

We didn't need anyone to say anything, yet people in the hundreds were a daily reminder that our son has passed. The intentions of people were good, it was just causing us to live in hurt and pain for longer. It was stacking to the losses we had already incurred from the divorce and the house fire.

The losses were starting to compound in my life. I had no answers of how to stop the bleeding in my spiral downward. I felt like I was becoming a magnet to terrible situations and the worst part was I didn't know how to stop it. I was at the point of asking myself the question, "What else?"

My son's death was another reminder of all that was not working well in my life. There was a huge gaping hole through my heart. Yet, at the same time I was losing it mentally. I knew I had to hold up our already broken family as the father and ex-husband, but had enough trouble getting out of bed in the morning from my increasing depression.

The Decision to Change

I returned home after all of the whirlwind of activity and faced a lonely house where more questions than answers existed. Old patterns die hard. I continued to have my couple drinks a night, several nights of the week. I ate dinner at late hours and had what was convenient to eat.

I felt I was no closer to understanding what my life had become and why. I was hitting a period where I felt like I couldn't take any more. I was overwhelmed. I had allowed myself to be disrespected by insensitive people at my job and it just added to the stress of all that had taken place. Work was an escape mostly due to the great nature of many of my colleagues, and from being in a position to mentor less experienced supervisors and handling the leadership development aspects. After I left work each night the silence echoed in my brain.

With so many devastating events in my life that seemed to be stacked on top of each other, my stress was out the roof, my health declined, and I abandoned so much of what was important to me in life. I was harsh to people in my personal life who didn't deserve it. I was imploding. It was time for a huge change.

I have since left the company that I was working for. My focus has been on my family and working on projects that inspire me. Drinking alcohol is a thing of the past and I am now a complete opposite of what I was just a few years prior.

This book will show you how I organized my life and acquired resources and lessons that would ultimately allow me to be where I am today. I am a complete 180 degrees from where I was. I have mastered the triggers leading to pain. I am at peace the majority of the time. I have a great relationship with my kids. I live my days and nights the way I choose to. I get to help others with challenges and improve people's lives. The future is inspiring and I have a strong management of my emotions on a moment-to-moment basis.

A relationship ending is painful. As much as I wanted the pain to stop, I needed time to figure it out so I could start living productively again. I know it is no easy task taking forward actions (like reading this book), when you feel terrible.

I promise to do all I can to cut the pain short and help to put a desirable future in view for you. Thank you for your faith in me and allowing me to share my path with you. I promise I will not bore you with statistics and science, though both are deeply imbedded in the answers and methods shared here. Let's get started!

Introduction

"Never allow someone to be your priority
while allowing yourself to be their option."
— Mark Twain

The chapters to follow will document the journey I experienced to get beyond the pain, insecurities, uncertainty, loneliness, and the sense of loss I experienced. There is a culmination of tools I utilized, educational resources that were monumental for me, and insights which can save recovery time. Anything that jumps that resonates with you, embrace it and use it.

Once I realized that the future was bright and the choices were unlimited, I was able to turn it all around. That was a difficult place to reach because I was stuck in negative emotions. Noticing opportunities for the future was just not a place I was ready to head toward. In other words, I wasn't going to shift until I was ready. By offering my path and lessons to you, the goal is to help you get to a better future with less pain and faster than you thought you could.

People ask why I would write a book on this topic since it was such a painful part of my life. My reason for dedicating my time to this topic is grounded in the fact that I don't want to see anyone else to experience pain at the level I was experiencing. I was miserable and if I can help get you unstuck via what I learned, I will certainly do my best to assist. My misery will only come by knowing I can help others and not doing anything about it. The message in this book is my way of helping you get past the hard times and enjoying life again.

The second reason for writing this book is knowing how completely free I felt when I moved from reactionary mode to proactive mode after the divorce. It was like lifting a heavy weight off my shoulders and getting a second chance to do it better.

The other distinction that struck me was that who you learn from can make a huge difference. When I was ready to make changes, I studied everything I could on intimate relationship recovery after a breakup. The largest struggle I had was trying to find information from someone who could relate to my situation. I found few people who had been in a 26 plus year relationship like I had, as a matter of fact many people writing on the topic had been in a relationship under five years and sometimes already had multiple breakups or divorces.

I also noticed that a large portion of the materials on the topic were written by counselors who had small setbacks compared to mine and wrote their books from a professional stance, or with client stories, and often only with classical psychology models. I did not buy into a complete program written by the mentioned writers. I did find some information useful but not enough to help me get to the place I was looking to arrive at emotionally.

Finally, I noticed most breakup books were focused on both the person dumping the other, and for the person getting dumped. The books address a breakup as a whole. The emotions and recovery are completely different. I wrote this book for only people who were on the receiving end that the relationship is over. In other words, this book is designed for the person who got dumped.

I turned a great deal of my attention to tools by people specializing in the various emotions I experienced, like fear, stress, and learning to let go. You will be exposed to most of the tools I used to move forward in life. I found that I needed to take action and try new approaches, or I would remain stuck in the pain. It was a requirement to do the work to get there.

This book focuses on my experiences and what worked for me. Some education is from other thought leaders in given topics I needed help with. I paid attention to tools that could make the largest difference in the shortest amount of time. It is common sense that some tools and ideas will work better for some people more than it will with others. There is no magic bullet that will be a fix it all for everyone. Again, there are those hungrier to learn and resolve their situations now, while others are not yet ready to move forward.

One of the major insights I stumbled upon was that my decisions and problem-solving abilities were greatly ineffective when the state of mind was in a stressed or hopeless place. I learned to change my mind in a hurry to remedy the weak mental solutions.

Tony Robbins mentioned that the best way to change the mental state we are in is to dramatically change physiology (getting the body moving), or to change our mental focus to a more productive place. When I was in a depressed state of mind I changed my breathing and posture, escaped for a walk, and changed the conditioned responses I was using. This was a huge tool for me in the recovery process. We will expand on this topic later.

It also helped greatly to know I was not the first person to go through this and certainly would not be the last. It wasn't that I wanted to see suffering on a large scale. Knowing that others recovered fully and went on to live better lives and more fulfilling futures was the medicine I needed. Pain and suffering is an extremely large blanket emotion but it is universal in the breakup process.

Grieving is also a universal topic and is something that most people will experience in life. I realized that I had to be able to experience the emotions without living in them. I had been living in the bad feelings of each emotion for way too long.

Denial will not work as it just pushes off the real issues that will exist following the breakup. If not confronted, one relationship after another will be impacted negatively. I am not stating that we should stay in the pain, but at least acknowledging it is a step in the right direction.

I assumed the victim role during and after my divorce. I was in a rut and felt powerless to change anything. I discovered the same thinking and behavior patterns were being utilized over and over. As mentioned previously, I hit a place where I said, "no more!" We all have an internal scale where we finally realize that staying stuck is more painful than just heading into action to change life.

The main goal of this book is to provide you with an extensive toolbox of ideas that can be used to customize or adapt to your situation. During the timeframe when I went through the transition from hard times to a more ideal life, I used a variety of resources and education to get there. There was no silver bullet, just finding things that overcame the negative feelings and offered a glimpse of hope for the future. Until I realized that it was all ok, and I could say to myself, "I've got this" I remained helpless and stuck.

When life seems bleak and we feel unlucky about the cards we have been dealt, we are actually in the best position to make huge shifts in our lives. When we are comfortable and life is on what seems to be the perfect path, people rarely seek to make changes. After losing a relationship, a job, or even a loved one when they pass, we often seek a new direction for life. You may not see it now, but the end of this relationship could end up being the best thing that after happened to you.

I will never say that time heals everything. After the death of our son, people would often state that time heals everything. I realized they were trying to help, yet I knew that they had not been put in the same situation. A friend of mine lost his dad, who was the closest person in his life. He said, "I finally realized that I would just never be ok with the passing of my dad." I agree fully.

I have learned that time helps us with a gap to learn to cope better when we experience times of personal tragedy. I would be the last person to tell you that time heals all when it comes to being abandoned in an intimate relationship. The important part is to learn to cope as quickly as possible so that new decisions and thinking can be utilized to design a better future.

When experiencing a breakup, many words of insult can fly back and forth between people. When the other person gives you negative labels it is hard to discard them from your mind. Stephen R. Covey, in the book, *Primary Greatness: The 12 Levers of Success* mentions, "When we disappoint or disagree with another person, we are often labeled and cast into that person's mental prison. We may cross over some sensitive line and hurt, insult, or offend another person. These labels tend to be self-fulfilling prophecies." Labels are thrown around carelessly, especially at the end of many relationships.

I know it hurts terribly now, but you are in the place to change what is coming in your life for the better. There is a path to a more fulfilling future if you choose to take it. The future can be meaningful beyond anything you ever experienced in the past.

I am looking forward to hearing your story of growth and change after it occurs for you. I will provide the best of what I have learned with the hope that it lights up some of your darkness and moves you into a positive place. I wish you all green lights ahead.

Chapter 1

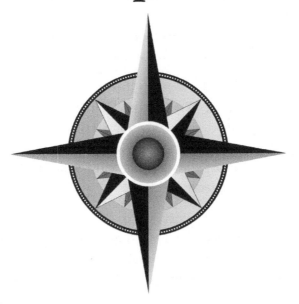

Book Map:
A Preview

"Life is one big road with lots of signs. So, when you're riding through the ruts, don't complicate your mind. Flee from hate, mischief and jealousy. Don't bury your thoughts, put your vision to reality. Wake Up and Live!"
— Bob Marley

We may never know why our spouse, boyfriend, girlfriend, or partner turned on a dime. Sometimes it is difficult to see the signs of a crash coming. We want to remember back to when love was fresh and it seemed unbreakable. We were in love and nothing could distract, yet end something that feels so perfect. The chances are that it could have been going in a negative direction for quite some time.

When my ex-wife and I were on the brink of divorce I previously mentioned a book called, "The Divorce Remedy" written by Michele Weiner-Davis. She discussed something called "Walk Away Wife Syndrome." After reading her section about this syndrome, I discovered a large part of why my wife and I were stuck and why she wanted out of the marriage.

Michele mentioned that two thirds of the divorces filed in this country are filed by women. She mentioned that in the early years of a marriage women tend to be the caretakers of the relationship. Women also tend to be more connected emotionally and evaluate the closeness of the relationship continually. They make judgments based on the evaluation of the ongoing efforts of their husbands.

What women consider concerns in the marriage can be perceived as "nagging" by the husband. Due to the lack of responses from their husbands, or even hostility they receive back, the wives become frustrated. The frustrations start taking form as complaints. These concerns and attacks go on for a while until the wives finally give up.

After several months or years of trying to get through to their husbands, the wives starting to plan a way out of a marriage and essentially "give up" trying. This a negative thing in the mind of the wife but the husband loves that the complaining stopped. At this point it becomes next to impossible for the husband to get his wife back emotionally because she made of her mind and is done.

I know that I experienced "Walk Away Wife Syndrome" in my marriage and I will not say that it was only my fault. I expected some fundamental shifts on her part too that I was not seeing. It was a stubborn standstill.

Regardless of how it happened, I was able to come to the realization after the divorce of exactly what had taken place. It is a little more difficult to see it when I stared it in the face each day. It is like having a child and everyone says, "Devon is getting so big." But because we as parents have been around him daily, we don't notice that he grew three inches in the last year. It is only after his physical with the doctor annually that we see the changes.

The signs are often there in a relationship that the direction is not productive but when two people are fighting to be right, we may never know why the other half shut off on a dime. We can use this tip for future relationships as a lesson.

The feeling of not being loved anymore is unbearable for many people. Not that it will put you at peace but I wanted to mention that the difficulty of disconnecting from your ex is not all your fault. You may ask, "Why can't I just get over her/him?"

First of all, a breakup consists of two minds and two people not being in alignment. Sometimes it goes way beyond the actions or behaviors of just one person. Just as recipes can often require certain ingredients in certain amounts, a relationship can require the same.

One example of relationship success and failure is the push and pull of the individuals in a relationship. If you are always the one pushing for the relationship to work and the other person doesn't carry his or her weight, there is little chance of long-term success in the relationship. The same happens when the other person takes more than they give. Even if a relationship continues with an unequal push and pull, the quality of the relationship will suffer.

A good portion of the difficulty in disconnecting from another is that your biology in the body causes the issue. In the *"On the Brain"* Newsletter from the Harvard Mahoney Neuro-Science Institute (Harvard Medical School Department of Neurobiology) in 2017, author Scott Edwards mentions a published study which used MRIs to test brain activity around love.

Love triggers increased levels of dopamine, which can create similar emotions and addictions to using cocaine or alcohol. If a relationship is newer the added chemical of cortisol, which is a stress hormone, comes with the pressure side of the relationship. This can lead to sweaty palms, a racing heart rate, and adds to compulsive behaviors like infatuation. The addiction you have may be more chemically driven than the perception of you thinking that you have something wrong with yourself mentally.

You may be asking, what the difference is in a long-term relationship in terms of these biological addictions? In 2011 Stony Brook University in New York conducted a study to do MRIs on couples married an average of 21 years. The same areas of the brain that are centered around dopamine activity continued to fire off, but with less stress since the relationship became more comfortable and predictable. So, again, chemical influences were involved and a breakup could create a biological tie to the partner who wanted the breakup. The lesson is that we are more involved with the person because of some level of chemical dependency. Don't be too hard on yourself with thinking you were stuck on a person like it was a will issue.

Knowing that that getting over the breakup is the goal, we still need to hold ourselves accountable for moving forward in life. We can start seeing that the future can be inspiring and fulfilling simultaneously. These two goals will be a focus in the book.

We will start from the beginning when the news of the breakup is delivered, and then can concentrate on moving toward creating a better life on your terms by the end of the book. To simplify the process I will be covering, the acronym R-E-S-T-A-R-T. Each chapter will start with a letter from RESTART.

If want to jump right to the tools without the need to get inside each topic, key insights are covered at the end of the chapters. It is recommended that you invest time to do the inner work included so you can recover on multiple levels mentally.

The areas of focus for the book are in *figure 1-1* to follow:

Reacting

Excuses and Denial

Separation

Taking Control

Adapting

Releasing and Surrender

Thriving

Figure 1-1

Chapter 2
Reacting: When It All Falls Apart

Reacting is the stage devoted to dealing with the initial knowledge of the breakup happening and the shock that follows. This is the time when you hear that the relationship is over. It is also when all of the emotions and body changes change as a result of the news.

Descriptions will be given for the emotions that are being experienced including the fear and uncertainty that come with being abandoned and having our hearts shattered. By the end of the chapter you will have some coping tools to handling negative emotions as they arise and removing many of the triggers that produce the emotions in the first place.

I associate my reinvention and transition from depressed to a new life as a form of portal I passed through. Before stepping into the portal, I had to come to complete honesty with myself and take full responsibility for the place I arrived at. I was angry at that point and wanted to blame everything outside of myself for the place I landed. I realized that I had to do the work to move on, I committed to passing through the portal, with hard work, until I arrived on the other side. Let's proceed to the components I conquered to pass to the other side of the portal.

In this phase, it is important to be kind to yourself and handle life moment-by-moment. There are just too many forces at work now and calmness (to the extent possible) is the best focus for the moment. Chapter 2 will go into detail of how to get to the calm state of mind.

Just plan that at this stage after the breakup, you will feel like you are going insane due to the large amount of emotions you are experiencing. The frequency and intensity remain to be seen, but right now the awareness that the emotions will be present and you are not going crazy, is what you will be experiencing as normal at this point.

As you will see from the pyramid on this page, to get to a life of thriving (at the top of the pyramid), there are areas that require attention before we can move forward and live a life on our terms. Make an effort to master each of the steps in *Figure 1-2*, which will be addressed in the chapters ahead, and a new life will be before you. I can personally say that this first stage of getting the news and learning how to deal with the ongoing negative emotions was the most difficult part for me. But I can unequivocally say you will get past it.

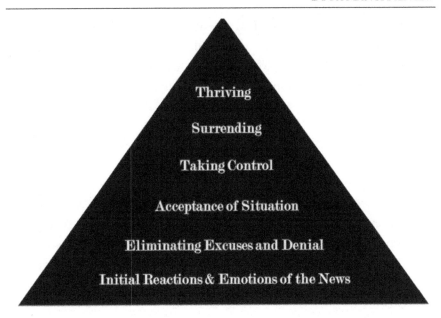

Figure 1-2

Chapter 3
Excuses and Denial: It Can't be Over!

Chapter 3 focuses on the *excuses* and *denial* that come after the initial shock. This is the chapter where we make key decisions that can produce personal growth, or keep ourselves in pain and suffering for longer.

We will discuss bargaining, trying to change ourselves for our partner, investing time writing letters, sending emails, tracking the ex's location, and making calls and hanging up. This is because of the loss of control or possibly trying to get our ex to talk. These are considered compulsive behaviors but are actually very common for many people who were dumped. Insights will be offered that can assist you in not pursuing this type of behavior, as well as the repetitive thoughts that go with them.

The goal of this chapter is to get away from the ex-partner so you can think on your own. A thinking gap is needed to reflect on your own emotions a bit versus obsessive thoughts about the person who left you. We must break the cycle of thinking about being triggered by memories of the person who left us. Any excuse of denial, about what is happening, is just keeping the thought and behavior loop cycling.

Chapter 4
Separation: The Reality Hits

This stage comes after the initial denial of the breakup. We continue to experience the negative mind and body numbing emotions after the breakup. At some point it becomes the reality of our situation becomes real for us. We realize that this is happening and we realize that there are some actions and decisions that must be immediately addressed.

When it becomes real we are finally empowered to start moving forward. It does not mean that we are supposed to be healed or making quantum leaps, it just means that we have accepted our reality for now and we are in a position to start turning the tide.

Being in a time that change starts happening is when we discover that we are either stuck, investing in the past, or doing something to control our current world. Advancing in our current world will create a different result in the future, so will accepting that we are stuck.

Chapter 5
Taking Control: Enough of the Pain!

After accepting that the breakup is a reality and knowing that we have to handle self-preservation and move on, the next phase is getting on our feet and getting out of the victim mindset if it still exists. This is the stage where we know action is a must and we have to get on our feet and not let more time slip away.

We will take the time to plan out, with clarity, what must be done to take care of immediate needs and eventually less vital needs that are still a "must" to complete. This is where we start gaining clarity about focusing on the solutions and getting off the problem. The ultimate goal is always to waste as little energy as possible on the problems, or what we cannot control. Saving the energy for solutions is a way to get to the end result faster. I have always tried to remember the saying, focus on solutions, not the problem.

Chapter 6
Adapting: New Habits and Philosophy

This chapter is all about adapting and conditioning our new rituals in body and mind. The pain is reducing and we now have ways of dealing with not only the pain, but also initial plans to move life forward. This is a vital time because it is determined whether we will stay in the productive momentum created or if we retreat back into a rut and old patterns.

The entire plan is to keep the momentum generating forward and the best way to achieve this is to follow positive rituals with intention until they build into habits that become automatic. Patterns, whether positive or negative, are created by thoughts becoming behaviors. At this point, it is vital we become aware of our thinking patterns so they can be reversed immediately if not serving us. Chapter 6 will address this topic.

Chapter 7
Releasing: Letting Go

Chapter 7 contains the ingredients connected to our personal freedom. This chapter discusses what it means to let go of the attachment to the ex that has haunted us for so long. Tools are provided about how to get on a path of understanding and forgiveness. The importance of surrender is explained. You will walk away from this chapter understanding the importance to self, and of being able to surrender and know that letting go is the best choice and vital to an inspired future.

Releasing a past relationship is more for *you* than for them. This chapter is about freedom emotionally that allows us to move on. It is not just people we are releasing, it is also to release ideas, personal rules, values, and philosophies that no longer are serving us. Life without constant pressure is a different world than keeping ourselves in prison over how we think we are supposed to be acting now.

I realize that releasing and moving on is not nearly as comfortable as staying stuck in a routine that has us in a tailspin. It requires us to step up to get out of the patterns. As Anneli Rufus described in her Book, *Stuck: Why We Can't (or Won't) Move On*, "getting unstuck, becoming free, requires vitality. Bravery. And enough honesty with yourself, about yourself, to change."

Chapter 8
Thriving: A New Life on Your Terms

The Thriving chapter is where the rubber meets the road. Up until now, mostly coping strategies have been discussed. There is a huge difference in coping and actually living your future the way you want to live. In Chapter 8 you will get to dream a little and make it ok for yourself to design a future that surpasses what you experienced prior. This is often a step of faith for you. The challenge becomes whether we stay where we are or we take additional steps that increase quality of life, in the way we plan and envision it.

Each chapter will contain important lessons or takeaways in case you are short on time to read all of the content in detail. There will be tools to use for handling each stage of the process toward crossing the portal. As mentioned prior, the main goal is to arm you with as many insights as possible to allow customization of your own plan that works for you.

The book will conclude with a master list of lessons I learned in my divorce that will hopefully make your life better now, and in the future. Many of the referenced lessons were difficult for me to learn and can be as good as gold to you if applied. It can also shorten the learning curve and get you feeling great again.

I was once told by a successful friend that just one insight from a book or audio can change it all in life. If a book is $15 and you get one idea that makes sense and changes your outlook and energy, it can be worth millions of times what was invested. Treat this book as a resource to turn to day and night, if needed.

I am an avid reader at the pace of two or three books a week. I buy the books, highlight key lines, and write in margins. I aim to *get from* the book and don't lightly peruse. I have collected insights that have shaken me out of my darkest hours and have inspired me to the peak of emotions. I hope the items on this list have the same impact on you.

With the intention of understanding divorce, breakups, splits, getting dumped, I will use the term ex throughout the book. This pertains to any form of the person the breakup or divorce happened with. Whether it is the ex-girlfriend, ex-boyfriend, ex-wife, ex-husband, the terms pertaining to the separation will be described in a variety of ways throughout this book.

One disclaimer vital to understanding before we move forward here, if you are under the care of a psychologist, psychiatrist, or medical doctor, please do not adopt the tools and strategies here to be a replacement of your treatment plan elsewhere. I utilized a huge variety of tools to reinvent my life after a divorce and many are not related classical psychology methods and may not contain approaches that are interwoven with an existing treatment plan. The results I experienced may be superior or inferior to the results you experience in your recovery. With the fine print out of the way, let's move forward.

Inspiration Checkpoint

Create a purpose and goal for transitioning to a life on your terms. Do not allow anything to distract you from that goal!

"If you do not change direction,
you may end up where you are heading."

— Lao Tzu

<u>Key Takeaways, Tools, and Lessons:</u>

Make sure to invest all you can in the processes described in the book. The healing increases exponentially when you invest in yourself

- If you choose to go straight to the key takeaways, tools and lessons at the end of the chapters, ensure that you are transitioning to better feelings inside. If not, you can go back and read the chapters and do the exercises

- It only takes one idea to inspire a huge shift in life that can change it all for you. If you own this book, I recommend using a highlighter and writing in margins. Get *from* the book and keep it as a companion

Part One
Crashing

"There is little that is more painful than the feeling of love slipping through your fingers. It hurts to wake up in the morning. You feel disoriented and dizzy. Nothing else matters. Your life, your thoughts, your feelings, your entire being is about your spouse falling out of love with you."

— Michele Weiner-Davis
Author of "The Divorce Remedy"

Chapter 2

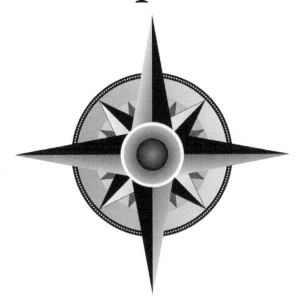

Reacting: When It All Falls Apart

"I can confront my fears with the knowledge that failure and rejection aren't fatal."

— Harold S. Kushner

"The pain of losing a person you love is part of life, part of this journey, but suffering doesn't have to be"

— Louise L. Hay

The shock of getting the news that a person no longer wants to be with us creates a web of hurtful emotions that we feel we can never escape. When we receive the news, it seems like time is standing still and disbelief is often the first emotion experienced. After it sinks in that this news is real, we are suddenly thrown into a black hole of negative emotions and triggers.

Of all of the stages after the breakup, this one holds the most emotional intensity and requires the best version of ourselves to address. The breakup brings triggers that are set off continually and the pain is still raw and continuous.

We run through our minds over and over about how this could have possibly happened. Keep in mind that no matter what was said about the reason for breaking up, it is always the result of two people.

I have seen and done my share of finger pointing and can tell you that the interactions and dynamics have a lot to do with a breakup occurring. Since it has been announced as over, we will need to run with the decision.

Initial reactions can be devastating. We are thrown into a sea of crashing waves mentally. It is normal to experience a range of negative emotions and thoughts including:

- Uncertainty

- How to live

- How custody of the kids will be handled (if kids involved)

- Loneliness

- The feeling of rejection

- Overwhelm

- Hopelessness

- Stress

- Anxiety

- Sadness

- Jealousy

- The huge hit to our confidence

It seems like triggers are present everywhere we turn and each reminds of the love we lost and adds to the emotional spiral downward. After my divorce, one night I had a shuffle playing on music and suddenly a song came on by "The Police". The song was *Every Breath You Take*. I am a guy who notices lyrics and I remember that night when a couple lyrics tore me apart, "Since you've been gone I've been lost without a trace. I dream at night, I can only see your face. I look around but it's you I can't replace." The emotions are triggered from everywhere including songs, pictures, places we frequented, cars that looked like hers, seeing her eyes in the kids, doing activities we shared at one point, to name a few.

From the details of my journey, you are aware of the range of emotions and experiences I went through and probably can relate to your own experience. How about you? Are you living one or more of these emotions? It is good to acknowledge and have awareness to where our current feelings and state of mind are so we can grow.

Some of my negative emotions intermittently continued for me for several months. I made the decision to be patient with myself and find compassion for my situation. That truly helped. The more we care about ourselves and take time to reflect on what is still good, it sure lessens the blow emotionally.

Since I had a jumpstart in knowing about the divorce, which some people don't have, I was able to start at least putting things in perspective in advance of the divorce taking place. Now, I know that I could have moved past the negative emotions faster. Tricks to helping you move quicker out of pain are covered in this chapter.

The goal for this chapter is not to remove 100 percent of your fears and emotions that are not serving you. Realism is part of the plan. The main goal is to get to what Dr. Joe Vitale calls, "Zero Limits." Joe states, "Zero Limits is about returning to the zero state, where nothing exists but anything is possible. In the zero state there are no thoughts, words, deeds, memories, programs, beliefs, or anything else. Just nothing." If you can get to a place that the mind isn't running wild and making life a complete catastrophe, then you have a better basis to move forward with.

I had a shattered vision of my relationship and of keeping my family together. I kept experiencing memories, mostly positive of my soon to be ex-wife, and of my family. Since our marriage had longevity compared to many couples, people used to ask me the secrets of a long-term relationship. Now that she asked for a divorce, I felt like any advice I had given was a lie since I couldn't make my own marriage work. At that time, I cared about what people thought of me and the breakup. The sense of judgment just added stress to an already overwhelmed life.

When we are in our heads about all of the things that are happening now, we limit the scope and quality of decisions we make and the possibilities we see for ourselves. Though it is opposite how we feel at this stage, a sense of calm is the best place to be.

If at all possible, take a step back and enjoy a calm breath of air. Try to see things from a bird's eye perspective now. The more we can outside of the situation, the better off we will be long-term.

We are often at the stage where we try to negotiate with the person who ended it. It may come in the form of phone calls, texts, emails, letters, checking up on them to see what they are doing, stating we love them, telling them all of the positives about the relationship, trying to get other people to talk to them (to clear his/her thinking), or purchasing flowers and gifts for them. All of these efforts can repulse them and can make them feel guilty for letting you go. Chances are, even if the person takes you back for the moment, it would be more about appeasing his or her guilt than actually desiring the relationship.

The efforts toward them also adds to your level of emotional despair and keeps the focus on something that is a dead issue to the other person. By controlling that urge it will allow you to think more clearly without the continuing rejection that is tied to your advances.

If they have said it is over, and they are serious about it, this is a great time for you to just find your own calm and start nursing the wounds so you can move on.

If it is not just denial about the end of the relationship, and you don't think the breakup is the end of it, I recommend you connect with the books and other products of Michele Weiner-Davis about saving your marriage. These are also tools you can try even if you were not married.

From my research, Michele has the most comprehensive set of tools to attempt to save a marriage or relationship. Don't let the title fool you since she targets the topic of divorce. The exercises and strategies can help in both marriages and any other type of relationship.

The good news about trying still is that you will know you did all you could do (within your power) to save your relationship and can move on knowing that. By trying the strategies listed from Michele, you will feel better about your own direction, which will help immensely if the relationship still does not work out.

If in your heart you know it is over, let's start the recovery process.

"At times when I am grounded on earth and see nothing but clouds, I try to remember: the sun is still there, always. I can't see it this very instant, but it doesn't stop shining, just because little me is on a part of the earth that is shielded right now."

— Michaela Haas

Dealing with Fear and Uncertainty

Fear and uncertainty are the two overwhelming emotions that hit right away when we are told it is over. With so much fear and anxiety of not knowing what to do, in what order, and being completely lost, I knew this had to be my first area to start working on.

With the voices in my head tricking me into "taking the bait" I spent a great deal of my time staying stuck in an endless circle of fear that I could not abandon. I confirmed that I needed my sanity quickly. I was reading a book by journalist Dan Harris with the irresistible title, *10% Happier: How I Tamed the Voice in My Head, Reduced Stress Without Losing My Edge, and Found Self-Help That Actually Works – A True Story*. Dan nailed it by stating, "The voice in my head can be a total pill. I'd venture to guess yours can, too. Most of us are so entranced by the non-stop conversation we're having with ourselves that we aren't even aware we have a voice in our head." According to Dan, it is an internal narrator that comes in the form of desires, judgments, urges, and is fixated on the past and the future.

With our existence up in the air because of the relationship shake up, fears, worries, and uncertainties are definitely going to be at the center of our worlds at this time. Our self-talk may be a main contributor to the focuses that are creating worry-some thoughts.

Keep in mind, it is very natural to feel this way and it is natural to think the worst right now, at least until our awareness catches the thoughts and emotions. Knowing that these situations will exist, it is better to have a way to plan for them in advance. It does not make problems go away but helps us better cope.

Fortunately, shortly after I was told about the divorce I was reminded about a book I had in my private library titled "*How to Stop Worrying and Start Living*" by Dale Carnegie. It is a classic and has some great steps to handle worry quickly and effectively. I will outline the steps, in summary, for you.

Step One:
What is the Worst That Could Possibly Happen?

Analyze the situations you worry about fearlessly and honestly. Figure out what is the worst that could possibly happen as a result of this situation. List all that you can think of that could possibly result due to this breakup. Get all of your most horrific thoughts out of your head on paper.

Step Two:
Reconcile Yourself to Accept that Outcome If Necessary

By accepting things if they turn out the worst possible, we can take the pressure off and own the situation easier. Even though the worst scenario rarely happens, commit now to accepting the situation if it does come true. By making this decision you unlock yourself to solutions that can improve upon these dire straits.

Step Three:
Devote Your Time and Energy on Improving on the Worst

From now forward, devote your time and energy to calmly to trying to improve upon worst relating to the situation that is causing worry. Come up with solutions and take action on the items with the most probable chance of working.

I took Dale Carnegie's advice and did the steps mentioned. I started by listing on the top of a pad of paper, in question form, what was the worst thing that could happen as the result of my marriage ending? The answers spilled out of my head and onto paper.

My list from the Dale Carnegie exercise included: I could get divorced, lose custody of my kids and end up with supervised visitation and be a loser father in life, lose the majority of my investments to my ex, lose my house, and have nowhere to live. I also listed potential bankruptcy and not have finances to live on. The thought came up that I would need to have two or three jobs to make it by. I thought about possibly having to sell my newer car and purchase a junker that would break down on the side of the road. I listed that I would never have money to go on dates or have to take my dates to Taco Bell and serve them off the value menu. I had visions of having to skip meals for days on end, for as long as possible. I had visions of being homeless and not recovering. The mind goes to horrible places yet we know it is more hopeful than the list we come up with.

My list was outrageous. The point is to mind-dump onto paper and get the fearful and worry-some thoughts onto paper so they are not just sitting in our conscious mind creating negative feelings for us. It is liberating sitting down and making this list because deep inside we know there is more hope than this.

For step two of the exercise, I wrote on another piece of paper that I was committed to accepting the above fate if that is what happened. Clarity existed for me that contained more hope and faith and there was little chance of it turning out this way, but it helped to commit to knowing the worst could happen that way if the planets lined up right. I felt in control knowing what I had to work with.

I then wrote at the top of another piece of paper in the same pad, "What can I do to immediately gain control of my life?" I started to then make plans of everything in my power to do that could ensure a better result than my depressing list. The most effective outcome of this exercise is that it gets a person on solutions quickly instead or marinating in the fear and worry for too long.

Our negative feelings are caused by negative thoughts. It comes from the mental state we are in at the time. Once in a negative mental state we must have a focus change if we want to think in a different way (to get better feelings). There are a couple ways to shift our focus and change our state of mind. It has been said that we can't fix a problem with the same thinking that was present when the problem was created.

Fear is like any other challenge in our lives to conquer. With your conscious mind telling you to just face your fears and your subconscious, or unconscious mind, habitually putting you into fear, we need to train the subconscious to assist us with making courage more automatic.

Fear can be reduced in the mind by visualizing more ideal outcomes. Brian Tracy, in his book, *No Excuses: The Power of Self-Discipline – 21 Ways to Achieve Lasting Happiness and Success*, he shares some valuable advice about repetition in visualizing successful outcomes. Brian mentions, "By visualizing yourself performing with confidence and competence in any area where you are fearful, your visual image will eventually be accepted by your subconscious mind as instructions for your performance. Your self-image, the way you see yourself and think about yourself, is eventually altered by feeding your mind these positive mental pictures of yourself performing at your best."

With the large level of thoughts that come through our minds a day, and how many thoughts are habitual day after day, we must consciously rise to the occasion of changing our states. With thousands of thoughts a day, with many are conditioned to re-appear over and over, how in the world are we supposed to catch unproductive thoughts and change our state of mind?

The easiest way to know when a state change is needed mentally is based on feelings. If we feel bad it is because our focus created a thought and the thought created a representation, creating an inner dialogue of what the thought means. The meaning generates an emotion that doesn't support us. So, the easy way to realize what we are thinking and focusing on is to notice how we are feeling. If we feel bad, we know it is time to change our focus immediately.

Inspiration Checkpoint

After feeling negative emotions initially, it is time to not own them anymore. Change your mental state and focus immediately by:

1. Change your body radically like a fast past walk or run or even running in place

2. Change your thoughts to what you DO have and feel deep gratitude

"People going through the anguish of love loss often feel that their lives have been permanently altered, that they will never be the same, will never love again. I'm writing to assure you that as devastated as you may be right now, your feelings of despair and hopelessness are in fact temporary, and they are a natural part of grieving over a relationship."

— Susan Anderson

Resilience and the Importance to Getting Back on Our Feet

The difference between resilient people and people who stay stuck for a long period of time is about the permanence level that is perceived regarding the challenges at hand. People often use phrases like, "This *always* happens to me." Or, "I can *never* keep a girlfriend." Notice the words always and never? Statements (labels) that tend to be all or nothing can be dangerous. Rarely is a situation all or nothing in our lives. Certainly, there are peaks and valleys and we are going to encounter *temporary* setbacks. That is part of being human.

Once we understand that these feelings and emotions are temporary it adds to our self-confidence toward solving the problems. The point is that the problems will change to solutions when we change our thinking and the depth we perceive our problems to be.

I remember reading years ago about how we all have peaks and valleys as a part of life. The resilient people who bounced back in a hurry have learned to maximize the peaks and cut the time they spent in valleys.

A great example of this, as Jim Rohn reminded us, is that we live in seasons. The most notable are summer and winter. If we do what we need to do in the busy summer season, the winters can be a down time and reliant on what we did all summer. An example is ants that scour for food all summer so that they have food for the winter. Can you imagine if ants decided not to "collect" all summer? There will be a problem in the winter.

Humans often do this with money. If we don't save in the positive summer months, when bad times come in life (winters) we will not have the resources to fall back on. We can always tell the people who did a great job maximizing the summers because they have the freedom to live in multiple homes during all the best seasons.

In relationships, there are also good and bad times, whether when involved in the relationship, or after it ends. When it ends, the regrets often begin. I should have done _____. I should have said _____. If only I would have _____. When it ends, it is good time to learn for next time. Learn to make the summers better down the road. Maybe winters will be shorter next time.

For now, realize the lessons that need to be taken from the experience and reinvent to something new and better. It is better to be a happy and fulfilled single person now than a miserable ex. It is a choice. Suffering really is optional in life. Believe me, I was in a place of needless suffering for a while. The sleepless nights, worry, focus on problems and not solutions, but I now know it was optional.

In, *Unstoppable: 45 Powerful Stories of Perseverance and Triumph from People Just Like You*, author Cynthia Kersey mentioned, "The one common link among unstoppable people is adversity – they struggled, tripped and stumbled, and had setbacks and failures, and they pulled themselves up and kept going." As Cynthia mentioned, "Adversity is a part of life and all we can do is lift ourselves up or go down in a sinking ship."

Cynthia Kersey outlined qualities of unstoppable people. Each element adds to the resilience level we will have at our disposal, when we are going through difficult times.

The Seven Qualities of Unstoppable People:

1. Devote themselves to their true purpose.

2. Follow their heart's passion.

3. Believe in themselves and their ideas.

4. Prepare for challenges.

5. Ask for help and build a support team.

6. Seek creative solutions.

7. Persevere, no matter the challenges.

We are in a painful stage at this point and asking you to make the leap to a happy single person is a stretch. There is a lot of processing to take place before arriving at the point of being at peace and functioning with emotional management.

Chaos is at the center of our universe right now. That is our reality but realizing the direction we are heading, and trying to find the peace with the pain will remain a key to internalize. Richard Carlson said something that has stuck in my mind. He stated, "To be truly transformed, we need to first learn to be at peace while we're in the middle of all this confusion. Usually we are doing one of two things: Either we are heading in the wrong direction or we are heading in the right direction." Each time I had a cloud over my head I stopped and asked, am I heading the right direction or the wrong direction? It was a continual reminder to get back on gratitude and positive action versus staying in the dumps for too long.

One way to see your situation as more positive and hopeful is to notice others in much worse situations than yourself. You might not see that right now because the immediate emotions, but there is a lot of light in front of you.

There are always stories that remind us that we are not the only ones going through hard times, and sometimes people with much worse situations remind us to look at our blessings. Bethany Hamilton, the professional surfer from Hawaii lost an arm in a shark attack. Actress Charlize Theron at age 15 witnessed her Mom shooting her Dad in self-defense. There are thousands of examples of people who have seen more tragedy in their lives than we will ever experience.

I was reading about actor Kelsey Grammar, star of the hit show Frasier. He lost his grandfather at a young age. He also lost his dad to a car fire. Someone lit his dad's car on fire and his dad was burned alive. Then Kelsey's sister was murdered. If that were not enough, his two half-brothers died in a scuba diving accident. This reminded me to always see how lucky I was to have what I have in my life. I lost a son, but I also had two other kids I could connect with. I lost a home to a fire but also had a fresh start after. When I see stories of tragedy, I feel for the people involved. The stories always help me with my personal perspective.

When I realized how difficult my life had become I tried to put it all in perspective after the situations like I mentioned. I still had my daughter (who is now 23) and my youngest son who is 11-years-old. My parents are still alive. I knew I had good friends. I realized the sun rises each day, darkness follows light, and then light follows darkness again. I was well aware that others do not have the advantages I have. I knew that there was someone somewhere suffering at a level I would never experience. This allowed me to more quickly get out of my unresourceful states.

Since you know how bad you have been feeling from the breakup, the rest of this chapter will focus on what we can do to gain productivity from here forward. The reaction phase after the breakup is the most difficult aspect of recovering. If you can dive in deeply to the tools provided, you should be able to find "pockets" of relief as you wade through the emotional mess right now.

One of the best investments we can make in ourselves at this stage is multiple pads of paper or spiral notebooks and good writing pens. There are several reasons why getting your thoughts and plans on paper is a good thing to do. First, it allows us to get all these lingering thoughts out of our minds. With the way we have been feeling recently, the last thing we need is our minds overflowing with regrets, unproductive emotions, and carrying an emotional suitcase everywhere we go. Having a place to write, whether on notepads or journals, gives us a location to transfer emotions out of the head and into a workable place.

Another positive aspect of getting thoughts onto paper, is it allows us a recording of what we need to face and work on. It is a written record of our scenario at hand and also gives us a platform to build ideas of where we are heading, which is the key to getting out of the mess we are experiencing currently.

The number of notepads I filled in my breakup years was an amazing sight to see. I bought tons of the Docket Gold Pads by Tops as they were super nice quality. I devoted the high-quality pads only to designing my future, or ideas about my future. Nothing negative or that contained negative emotions was written on the Docket Gold pads.

I also stocked up on the 70-page one subject spiral notebooks each year when they were on sale for 19 cents each. I also bought the Home Depot in-house brand quality pads. I believe they are called "Office Depot Professional." They were more cost efficient than the Docket Golds and had double the pages. I purchased Pilot G2 gel pens by the dozen as my pen of choice to use in my self-work.

I will share with you what I used the paper for. For now, it might be useful to have paper and pens ready to capture ideas and mind dump as needed right now while thoughts are racing through your head. It can help you clear some of the mental overwhelm you are experiencing. It is like when we speak and we get things off our chest to another person, but on paper it is your own private world. Solitude, to an extent, can be your friend right now. Time is on your side and right now it is all about taking care of yourself and your needs.

After purchasing tons of notepads and spirals, the first strange topic that came to my mind was whether all the labels ever given to me by my ex-wife, via fights or compliments, were true. I am not sure why that was so important to me as first steps.

I wrote down everything I could remember, good and bad, that my ex-wife had said about me over the years so I knew what I needed to work on for the future. It is hard to trust all of the things I said to her or that she said to me. Labels may be inaccurate due to being made in the heat of battle and are not meant for anything but hurt when times are difficult in the relationship. I made a list of all the negative aspects about myself that were mentioned and made another list of positive qualities that were mentioned.

After brainstorming years of labels, I gave copies of my lists of both good and bad qualities to some trusted friends who would level with me and would honestly assess my strengths and weaknesses. The answers came back almost identical from each of my friends. I knew what changes I needed to make based on the feedback. I wrote down action steps to improve each of the areas of weakness so I didn't carry them into future relationships. It has taken years to condition some of the unproductive qualities into a more productive counterpart.

Another tool that helped me immensely was keeping "Inspiration" journals. Any time I had an inspiring thought, I grabbed a spiral notebook and wrote down that thought. I filled up 29 notebooks of 70 pages each (single space college-rule) in just the last several years.

I noticed that even though I spent time in fear and anger I also had flashes of elated pictures in my mind about my future. One image that came to mind was sitting by a beach in Maui with breezes hitting me while enjoying the sounds of crashing waves close by. Another thought was sitting with my son having movie night together and seeing him smile and yell out when there was a "cool" part of a movie.

The inspiration notebooks have provided me a positive energy-charged tool to turn to when my mind was focused on only bad thoughts. To feel the inspiration even deeper, I typed the inspiring thoughts from the notebooks into the computer. The feeling was incredible. It was difficult not to be elated during the process as I was visioning each item as I was typing.

Bouncing back for me also came through understanding why it was so important that I get back on my feet quickly. For me, my kids were the purpose. I wanted to accelerate my way out of pain quickly so they didn't see me upset consistently. They didn't deserve the backlash of my marriage falling apart. They are just kids.

People often ask me, "How am I supposed to put on my best face for my kids when I feel like crap myself?" I have to answer in the only way I know how, which is my own perspective and experience. I had dark thoughts and had a huge level of uncertainty, but when my kids were awake I needed to check on them and see how they were doing. I put all my focus and presence on them whenever I could. I didn't want to lose the mental and emotional connection with them just because of a breakup.

WARNING

Try to avoid going to family members and friends if they tend to interject their own opinions without being objective about your situation. Some opinions are more productive than others.

Sometimes our friends and family think they are helping by telling us what "a jerk he/she was" or adding more fuel to the fire than what is needed. These opinions and remarks can greatly slow your pace to healing. Too many people want to stir the hornet's nest or insert their opinions when they may be the worst person on the planet to be giving relationship advice. I'm sure the intention they have is the best for you, it is just easier to take advice from only people who have a good track record to offer the advice. Otherwise, it can prolong the pain.

You don't need any more negative emotions now and you will get sick of hearing from the people in a hurry. If they give terrible advice or suck your energy, you may want to rid them from your daily contacts you are surrounded with.

Listened to a Podcast from Tim Ferriss about getting life down to the essential 20 percent of the activities and people that bring 80 percent of your results or fulfillment in life. He said to ask ourselves, "What are the 20 percent of people in life that bring us the most stress and anxiety?" He said to resolve to pull those people from your consistent exposure. That is great advice with so many voices already going through our heads!

Change your language and speak about all of the positive things that can happen due to your change in situation. Positive thoughts have huge healing power and when we say them to ourselves and others, we reinforce that it is all going to be better than we ever expected.

Handling Anger and Rejection

Anger as defined by Merriam-Webster dictionary is a strong feeling of displeasure and usually of antagonism. When we were discarded in a relationship we can be stuck in a feeling of uncertainty about the outcome of our situation, and it is natural to blame the other person from the relationship for the predicament we are now in. Anger can also be due to our ideal visions of the relationship for the future, and our expectations not being met by our ex-partner.

Anger is natural after getting rejected and filled with uncertainty. It is an emotion that can lead to some terrible consequences in life if not conditioned back to neutral. This section will give you some tools for handling anger and leave you feeling more empowered than prior.

Neuro-Linguistic Programming

Anger is usually triggered mentally as a self-protection mechanism. We are refusing to be dumped and left to pick up the pieces. It is a fight against the rejection we experienced. It can be tied to the fight or flight response, where we stay and fight or leave the scene. We are in a fighting mood as we perceive that we were taken advantage of.

One of the tools that has helped me tremendously is called Neuro-Linguistic Programming (or NLP for short). I know it sounds like a complicated science, but in reality, uses steps of thinking to figure out the final result that we are receiving. We can then step back and determine how our patterns are formed and then how to break the pattern. A better explanation is shared in the book, *NLP: The Essential Guide – Creating the Person You Want to Be* by Tom Hoobyar,

Tom Dotz, and Susan Sanders. The authors shared, "NLP is based on the theory that all human thinking occurs in pictures, sounds, feelings, smells, and/or taste: the five senses. In other words, we create recipes, in order, of the five senses to establish a certain result.

Many people, when hearing about the seeming complex nature of NLP shun the idea of it working, or take on the belief that they can't learn it. It is one of the fastest ways and offers one of the most powerful and lasting ways to deal with negative emotions and patterns in life once we learn it.

We all have our own tendencies to lean toward one of three main senses, which is a visual sense, and auditory sense, or a kinesthetic sense. In simple terms, a person with a visual sense talks in pictures and learns from things they see, or in combination with other senses. An auditory favored person, gets more from talking and conversation or reading. A kinesthetic favored person tends to learn from doing and experiencing situations in the way that they feel. Without getting too complicated, it is good to learn the basics of Neuro-Linguistic Programming.

People who prefer visual as a preference tend to talk quickly as they want to describe a picture before it goes away in their head. An auditory learning and preferred person will use words like, "I will *talk* to you later." Kinesthetic people speak slower and like to feel the situation, and are hands on in learning as they want to try something and not watch or listen.

When it comes to the topic of anger, NLP can describe the sensory experience we have that creates anger in our minds. Tom Hoobyar, Tom Dotz, and Susan Sanders state, "When someone has a sudden scare or flash of anger, it triggers a reaction in the body. Their bloodstream is flooded with hormones and chemicals. Their heart races and their eyes narrow. Their breathing increases and they get ready to fight or run away. Chemicals like these go into the brain and change the way it works. Then those parts of the brain devoted to higher functions, like creative thought, shut down and other, more basic parts take over. When this happens, you become a specialized survival machine." In other words, when we are triggered by a thought or event, our minds are in fight or flight response and we go into a habitual state of mind that does not allow clear thinking.

Where NLP comes in handy is when we understand how to use these senses to our favor to lessen anger (and other negative patterns). Let's say you are more visual then the other senses. If you are visual and heavily rely on pictures to create your reality, we can tune our pictures to be more or less appealing. A person with visual preferences will be more motivated, or angry, when they turn up the brightness and clarity of the pictures in their minds. So, if you have a picture of anger after being triggered, you may have an image of what the other person did to you, clearly established in your mind. If your picture is vivid and the colors and brightness are sharp, and you increase the size of the image in your mind, like a movie screen, you will intensify your levels of anger. If you take the same picture in your mind, make it smaller, turn it to black and white and turn down the brightness, you will not react with so much passion. You can change your "recipe" and get a different result.

I will share a tool from NLP that you can start to use immediately to deal with a negative emotion that is causing you problems. It is called the Swish Pattern. It is a different pattern depending if you are more visual versus auditory. Keep in mind that even if you are auditory in approach, some emotions like anxiety, irritation, fear, and jealousy that contain more energy, tend to be oriented in a visual way. If you feel depressed or feel down sometimes these lower level energy states come from an inner voice (auditory cues). So, you can try both the Auditory Swish Pattern and the Visual Swish Pattern and see which one works better for you anytime you encounter negative experiences.

Auditory Swish Pattern

Before the Exercise:

Listen for an inner voice that causes a loss of confidence or discourages you from taking an action. These are voices that could have been conditioned into you from years prior. Go inside your mind and notice what the voice is that you are hearing. Step into the feeling that you are experiencing and the words that you are telling yourself from that emotion. It could be a voice saying, "This isn't possible." Or "I can't win no matter what I do." Notice if this voice is coming from in front of you, behind you, from the side, as we tend to usually generalize and think it is all centered.

Is it your own voice or one of a parent or another authority figure in your life? These voices were recorded at an earlier time. Sometimes the voices came like they are being spoken right at us from the front when it is in the form of self-talk. If it is a voice coming from others it tends to be coming from behind us or to the sides, or even from above. These are usually repeated comments like, "Wow, you are lazy" or something that just seems to linger in your head. With these initial ideas of the voices, try the process below (which is shortened in the interest of space) but can be effective.

Step One:

Get your mind to hear the voice, and right when you hear it, grab your internal volume control and turn down the volume until the voice quickly fades out. It is best to not even let yourself complete one word before the volume is muted completely.

Step Two:

Create an image of yourself, but the image is in front of you and you are looking at you. This is the *future* you. When you look into the eyes of the future you, the person is definitely you but this "you" does not have the same voices you have. Then take notice that they are saying something to you. The future you is saying, "I feel great about who I am" or "I am safe and feel secure." You choose the statement that feels right to you and let the statement ring around your head. It is circling around or above your head or eyes and you hear the statement that resonated with you over and over again. You really hear it this time. This is you, just with positive voices. You just notice it is really you there with no negative voices.

Step Three:

Now allow the sound of the surf to wash away the sounds of the negative voices. Each time you hear the negative voices now, all you hear is your positive statement, and it is repeated over and over, then the sound of the surf knocking off any negative edges remaining. So, it is a matter of replacing the negative with the positives, but doing so in a way that you can distort the message and volume.

Now I will outline the visual version of this pattern. The visual version is good for you if you had intense images during the last exercise. It is important to notice what has an impact on you. Let's try the Visual Swish Pattern.

Visual Swish Pattern:

Step into your mind and find a picture of something that causes you emotional turmoil and what the situation or trigger for that emotion is. For example, if you are angry at your ex and you explode at your family members each time your anger is triggered by your ex, then address that situation. Choose something that you know if hurting you now and get that image in mind.

Step One:

Take the large picture of what you don't want and imagine all the negative details, like the look on your face and the anger you are experiencing in detail. See all the negative things in the picture that you no longer want in your life.

Next, form a new mental image of you acting the way you want ideally and create a small picture with all the details of what that looks like. This will be the new image of you performing that act perfectly. Tie pride and self-worth into changing to the new picture.

Step Two:

Close your eyes.

Blow up the negative image you decided on to be big in your mind and put an angry colored background like red behind yourself doing the negative behavior. You can even turn it into a video if you like in your mind.

Next, put a small, dull, green background picture of what you see as the perfect scenario in the bottom right corner of the larger unwanted image.

Step Three:

With your eyes still closed do the following:

Do a linkage of the two images, positive and negative. See the picture of what you don't want and then grab the green background picture of what you do want with your hand and bring it up over the bigger red background image and grow the green wanted image brighter and larger and explode it over the red unwanted image. Blow up the red image in your mind as the green one takes over. As you are doing it, say the word, "Swish!" and see the new one in control now.

Step Four:

Repeat this process until the new empowering image automatically takes over the old negative image. Keep doing this until all you see is the new image. Condition in the new image until you do it automatically.

The original processes were developed by Richard Bandler, who is one of the originators of NLP. Neuro-Linguistic Programming allows a person to take lifetime patterns in the mind and body and eliminate them within minutes. I will list some tools about NLP in the resource section of this book.

Triggers and Mental Anchors

Our most intense emotional experiences, whether positive or negative, tend to get stored as triggered memories. For example, do you have a smell that causes you to step back right into a time 10 years prior? Or, have you heard a song and it triggered your mind back to a specific experience where the song was playing? We anchor memories to emotions consistently. We love the positive triggered emotions but unconsciously react to negative ones as well. I will share examples of how mental anchors work to generate emotions in us.

My close friend Annette visits often and we like to sit out on my front porch under the stars when she is here in the evenings. In Colorado, the weather can get extremely cold, or cooler and breezy, so sometimes we partially open the garage and sit out there when it is too cold on the porch. I have a garage light with a motion sensor and shuts off if motion is not detected. Sometimes I forgot to turn on the main light in the garage, so we relied on the motion-activated one.

After about five minutes the light would shut off and I would raise my arm to activate it again to turn the light on. We would be in the middle of a conversation and the light would go off and she would watch my arm or arms going up, like doing the wave at a stadium, and she started laughing hysterically. To this day, a year later, I can just raise my arms in the same way and Annette will start laughing until she is in tears from laughing so hard. It doesn't matter where we are, as it works no matter what. That is a positive anchor that can be triggered. Any time Annette is down about something, which isn't often, I can just raise my arms and it puts her in happy mood.

The same mental anchor can happen for negative emotions and situations. It has been just two years since my son passed away at the time I am writing this, and I still have trouble going to the cemetery to visit his gravesite. Though I had positive memories with him throughout his life, the last memory I have of him in the physical world was him being placed in the ground and all of the people standing around as we cried and said goodbye. Though it was a painful day, and the concept of a soul versus a body is in play, if I go to the cemetery and stand by his grave, I instantly trigger into sadness. I get a range of emotions in my mind that flow like a river when I am there. For this reason, I have an easier time having a one-directional conversation with him on my porch at night versus triggering the terrible feeling I have by going to the cemetery.

I modified how I handle many of my triggers, including situations that placed me in an angry state. Now I am to a place where I have zero anger toward my ex-wife, which is a huge cry from when I perceived her as the devil for breaking up our long-term marriage and family. Today, my ex-wife and I can easily turn to each other for help and we know the other will be there.

This is a scenario that re-conditioned over time. There were simply too many anger triggers early to even talk for five minutes without fighting being the outcome of every discussion. Every time I left her house I could feel my heart rate racing and I kept that anger for the entire evening. It was a wakeup call to me when I went to my doctor and he took my vitals and ran my blood. I asked myself: "Is this anger worth dying for?" Obviously, the answer was no. I sat and wrote out all of the things she did that I allowed to trigger anger in me.

I also looked up the effects that anger has on people if we don't let go. I knew I could feel changes in myself each time I was in a state of anger. I also knew I needed leverage in myself to stop allowing it to happen. Dr. Joseph Mercola, a prominent health expert and widely published advocate of natural health, mentioned the impact of the automatic anger response leads us to health problems including:

- Insomnia

- Heart Attack

- Headaches

- Skin problems including eczema

- Digestive challenges

- Stroke

- Depression

I was concerned with already declining health, and anger was just adding to my problems. My dad had a stroke not so long ago and when I saw strokes on the list of repercussions of anger, I knew I better take a step back and view anger from a larger picture. Not only was I eating up my time and energy in life by staying mad, but I could die from it. It was keeping me from living my own life. She wasn't even with me anymore and I was upset during MY time? Wow, what a wake-up call!

In addition to declining health issues from anger, it also negatively impacts us mentally like fear does. It blinds us from making intelligent choices in life and limits the amount of solutions. When serotonin levels lower in the brain from the presence of stress, anger increases. Lowering stress can help to keep serotonin from decreasing, which lowers the chance of aggressive behavior, like anger.

One of the natural ways to raise serotonin in the brain, per the National Institute of Health is to get bright light (like sun each day).

This is a good mood enhancer and is easy to accomplish. The life expectancy in Hawaii is higher than the rest of the country. According to Dr. Bradley Willcox from the University of Hawaii, from the John A. Burns School of Medicine, "You get vitamin D from the sun when you're outside, and it's easier to be physically active here – you're not dealing with two feet of snow for a good chunk of the year." Even if you don't have the luxury of moving to a stress-reduced tropical paradise, get outside and get some sun.

Exercise creates increases in serotonin in addition to sunlight. Even if you get out and take walks when possible, it helps rid of bad moods and aggressiveness. The more aggressive you feel, the more you should incorporate movement and physical fitness.

Diet is also a contributing factor to serotonin increases or decreases. Tryptophan is the ingredient that produces the most in increases. The debates still exist whether it is better to get the supply from food or from in drug or pill form. Just try to add try Tryptophan.

The final way to impact serotonin positively in the brain is through thought modification. This is the focus of this book and can happen as a result of the exercises we will be going through in the chapters ahead. The focus on hope and faith are a great starting point to modifying thoughts.

Expect that rage will come and go. One second we can be sad and thinking about a host of other subjects in our minds, and suddenly the anger sets in. This is a normal response. The mind is not very focused at this stage and will continue to jump all over, so don't label it as a challenge of the self. Just do all you can to keep mood higher right now.

On a pad of paper, or in the notes pages in the back of this book, if you own the book, please take a minute and get awareness to what triggers anger in you. At the top of a page you can write, "What, when I think about it, makes me angry about my ex?" Write your answers.

The next step is to come up with 1-2 or more ways that you can respond differently, then using anger, when confronted with those situations. The goal is to not have an overnight cure to anger, but to reduce some of the negative impact you are experiencing because of it.

The same tool to neutralize anger triggers can be done with every emotion you are experiencing that is causing you pain. It is good to invest the time to complete a trigger inventory so you have ways of dealing with emotions that arise from time, place and situation.

Rejection is a different emotion completely. When we assume the rejection, and own it inside, it can take a toll on the self. Keep in mind that we stack all of life's rejections on top of each other to create a compound effect on self-esteem. Being abandoned in life creates the feelings of rejections, or in other words a mental representation of what the abandonment means. When you are looking at the abandonment by your ex-partner you are only experiencing the tip of the iceberg of what other rejections have handed you.

Self-doubt and worthlessness feelings arise and without going back to the start of all of the abandonment and rejection feelings, it will be difficult to clear it all. We have to re-engineer the self-image. The resource that helped me the most with this challenge is called, *The New Psycho-Cybernetics: A Mind Technology for Living Your Life Without Limits*. By Dr. Maxwell Maltz and Dan Kennedy. The mentioned version is an audio series released by Nightingale-Conant. The premise of this program is that the self-image either allows an expanded life or keeps us in self-doubt and limits. This audio series is also good for stress-reduction.

The other source that was extremely helpful for me around the topic of abandonment and rejection is by author Susan Anderson. Her book, *The Journey from Abandonment to Healing: Surviving Through and Recovering from The Five Stages that Accompany the Loss of Love*, focuses on all of abandonment, not just intimate relationships, but was a huge awakening for me. Her book deals with the process of grieving and compounded abandonment issues. I had several I did not consider before reading her book. My mother leaving my brother and I at various times when we were kids was one of my first remembered abandonments. Susan reflects on rejection in her book. She explains, "One of the primary tasks of abandonment recovery is to prevent feelings of self-doubt from adhering to your sense of self."

I knew that after reading Susan Anderson's quote about self-doubt adhering to my sense of self, I had to make it a goal to see the rejection and attacks toward me as a factor of the external relationship instead of me being a bad person. I stopped listening to the negative and simply placed the blame on factors that happen in life. This was my way of being gentler with myself and avoiding additional damage to my self-esteem.

Some Insights That Changed My Life

Everything in Life Consists of Energy

In my quest to improve my current situation and life forward, I came across the study of quantum physics. What struck my curiosity about this topic was that I realized that everything on the planet is made of energy.

We all vibrate at different frequencies, but nonetheless all frequencies are tied to energy. I knew that with focus change, body movement, or a number of other changes, I could raise my energy vibration and thus my internal feelings.

I came across a book that focuses on using energy management over time management. In Jim Loehr and Tony Schwartz's book, *The Power of Full Engagement*, the authors reminded me that, "The more we take responsibility for the energy we bring to the world, the more empowered and productive we become." This insight changed me because I realized that in the grand scheme of life, since everything is energy, it would be a best practice for me to master my own energy and bring it to the world.

I discovered an effective way to accomplish a better energy was to ensure I was consistently adding new knowledge to my arsenal of tools to help me. Growth is vital even when we feel we are dying inside. Knowledge is the enemy of fear. The more knowledgeable we are about a subject that scares us, the more in control we feel, which reduces fear.

One of my new practices in the past several years is to take my youngest child, Devon, on a trip to Hawaii with me once a year. This gives me a chance to connect with him, one on one, which means a lot after the death of my other Son Dylan. I felt I knew Dylan really well but as he aged he distanced. He stopped talking about things that were true concerns. I didn't want this to happen with my younger child.

My goal with Devon is to be present emotionally as much as I can. This has become a good practice When I go for a full week or two with him to Maui, and it is only the two of us there 24/7 real conversations take place. He has shared mounds of information with me that I was unable to get out of my other son in the past.

This year's trip to Hawaii (June 2017), it hit my awareness that he is growing up so quickly. He had his carry-on ready to go with his music, drawing pads, pens, books to read, and he spent a great deal of the longer part of the flight from San Francisco to Maui working on his own interests. I knew we could re-convene once we landed in Maui.

I took two books with me to read during the trip. The first book has the title, *The One Thing: The Surprisingly Simple Truth Behind Extraordinary Results*, written by Gary Keller and Jay Papasan. The second book was, *The Art of Living* by Bob Proctor and Sandra Gallagher.

I decided for the five-hour flight from San Francisco I would read the book with the best chance of finishing during the flight, so *The Art of Living* was my pick. Chapter 7 is called, "You Are the Sum Total of

Your Thoughts." Bob and Sandra stated, "You don't attract what you want. Wants are intellectual in nature. Wants are in your conscious mind. You attract what you are in harmony with, what you are." I realized that my presence with my son was changing my energy vibration and putting me in harmony with him. I also realized I could do this with positive intention for any other situation. That is a huge lesson when times are rough.

No Matter What, It Will All Be Great

I was perfectly whole and content before I met my wife, so why wouldn't I be after a divorce? That was a question that opened my eyes. Yes, my ex-wife was a huge part of my life, but I was also a huge part of hers. I realized that I had tons of experiences that were before her time that made my life a great experience. I had friendships that have weathered years. I served our military and traveled the world, and I had relationships with beautiful women (both inside and out). I earned three college degrees. I have gorgeous children and I can still be with two of them on a consistent basis.

I keep a huge gratitude list with me at all times as a reminder for how fortunate that I am. Not only did I list gratitude for what I have now, but also have items from the past and potential for the future. This helps to shortcut my thinking about what is missing or what I am hurt by. It isn't possible for the mind to hold and negative thought if a positive one is already on the mind.

There is Limited Time in This Life. Live It!

I realized that I had lived almost 48 years already at the time of my divorce and I can't for the world remember where all the time went. I only had limited time in this life and didn't want to waste it.

In the book, *New Beliefs, New Brain: Free Yourself from Stress and Fear,*

Lisa Wimberger mentioned, "Our lifespan is merely a blip on a screen of vast earth and space history. We have a choice in how we want to spend that precious time. Some of us yield to pain, punishment, stress, and anxiety; others fight hard to choose joy, love, and compassion." In other words, do we spend time in the negative aspects of life or would we like to live in a more beautiful mental and physical state the majority of our time here? It is a choice, but must be made as an unbreakable decision.

Withdrawals and Deposits

Life is nothing more than an emotional bank account. We are either making deposits in the account or taking withdrawals from it. Stress, worry, fear, rejection, blame, anger, overwhelm, indecision, jealousy, and host of other emotional states of torture were simply withdrawals from the account. Meaning, purpose, happiness, peace, daily action, joy, contentment, enjoying the moment, and the range of positive emotions were all deposits. Simply put, I decided to start making huge deposits and very few withdrawals. I made the decision to stop worrying, stressing, and living in fear about a situation that was not going to change.

I Was All I Had: Treating Myself Better

I was extremely hard on myself. I knew I had been a great husband, even with my shortcomings. I knew I was a good dad to my kids. I knew that 99 percent of what I was feeling now had to do with my identity wrapped up into a relationship that had consumed almost 30 years of my life.

It would not be an overnight process to establish myself as an independent and self-sufficient person again. I had a realistic optimism about where I was heading and knew that I had to give myself a break to breathe and establish a thinking gap. This keeps me from entering Catastrophic thoughts.

"A problem solver with the wrong mindset will miss the rich opportunities hidden in crisis, turned back when persistence might win the day, fall victim to the vulnerabilities, except unnecessary sacrifices, and never discover what can be accomplished by pushing one's own limits."

— Christopher Hoenig

I have to admit that there were times that I treated my breakup recovery as a project to take on, just like other projects I may do it at work or nonrelated to relationships at all. Christopher Hoenig, author of the book, *6 Essential Secrets for Thinking on a New Level: Making Decisions and Getting Results,* reminded me, "Developing strong ideas is the first, and in many ways the most crucial phase in the problem-solving journey." I came to the truth that if I wanted to get out of pain faster I would need to focus on the elements of this journey that I considered problems to solve.

By treating this as a problem-solving focus, I was able to remove the nerve-bending emotions that were caused by being in just a reactionary mode. At this miserable point in my life, I was willing to try anything to push past pain and get to a calmer existence.

The entire goal of this chapter was to give you some solutions that could help in coping with the pain of a fresh wound. Each tip offered was tried and tested by me to get to where I am today. Take all the time you need to create a plan, based on your thoughts, combined with any tips that I offered that fit your style and strike inspiration in you.

Key Takeaways, Tools, and Lessons

- The goal is to move past quicker and get to a neutral emotional state that doesn't have to be either negative or positive

- When staying in the rough thoughts we add to stress and decision-making quality is greatly limited. Possibilities and solutions are also lessened in this state of mind

- Stop the chase if pursuing your ex. It keeps your focus on the ex and reminds you of the negative you're experiencing

- If it is over, find the calm and create a gap to process your thoughts. Breathe and focus forward

- Think of what the worst possible scenario is for you now with the news you received. Then place all of your effort to improve upon the worst. Get a pad of paper and write the question, "What is the worst thing that could happen as the result of my marriage (relationship) ending? Write everything you can think of. Then at the top of another page, write the question, "What can I do to immediately gain control of my life?" Focus fully on this exercise to multiply options

- Change your negative mental state of mind by either radically changing your body, even if breathing at a rapid pace or changing what your focus is on. Frame your thoughts productively and have gratitude

- See the situation as temporary and something you will move through. Don't ignore it or deny it, but know that resilience starts with removing permanence from the situation

- Think of people in worst situations than your own and try to find the good and gratitude in what you have currently

- Get pads of papers, or spiral notebooks to journal thoughts and answer questions with. Purchase some writing pens to use

- Keep inspiration journals (spiral notebooks) and write down any inspiring thought that arises and turn to the journal when you are not feeling great. If you choose, type all of the journal entries into the computer to run your mind through positive thoughts

- Avoid family and friends who will stir the hornet's nest. If people have not had success with the area of challenge you are going through, or tend to give stressful and bad advice, don't talk about your issues with them. Also, think of the 20 percent of people and situations in your life causing you the most negativity and stress and rid of them from your consistent experience

- Put your focus on consistent growth and knowledge. Knowledge is the killer of fear

- Have presence in each situation you are in and keep the energy focused there

- You were fine before your ex (most likely) and you will be again. Focus on what you have done prior then focus on the future

- Think of your current situation as an emotional bank account. You either are taking withdrawals by focusing on Negative thoughts, or you are making deposits by staying on solutions and positive thoughts

Chapter 3

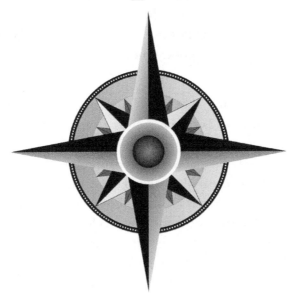

Excuses and Denial: It Can't Be Over!

"As you continue along this journey, you will perhaps be surprised to discover that the pain you feel when a loved one has left is not an end but the beginning of a time of personal growth"

— Susan Anderson

I knew when enlisting in the Navy that I would lose freedom, which is one of my most important values in life. My father was in the Navy and I enjoyed seeing all of the slides of the pictures he took while on his adventures. I loved the prospect of seeing the world and being able to do it all while having the pride of serving my country. I was basing my decision on the good times he showed me during his time in the Navy.

Once I was serving the Navy, it seemed cold and dark, and suddenly I was thousands of miles away from my friends and family. It wasn't like today when emails can be sent. If I wrote a letter to friends or family, it would take weeks or more to get to them and then just as long, or longer, if they didn't take the time to write in an expedited way. It was lonely, I was enlisted and low on the chain of command, which meant for some low levels of freedom. There were months when I didn't have a day off. I was done with active duty in 1988 and though at that time I couldn't wait to get my honorable discharge, today I remember mostly the good about the situation.

This story is applicable because we often try to recall all of the special positive memories of time with our exs, which is great if they wanted us and wanted to save the relationship like we wanted. Just as I kept positive memories of the Navy, there were also a lot of negative times that would get me to have second thoughts of doing it over if I could. When you sensationalize your ex, they are getting your energy even if they don't give an ounce of energy to the thought of you. When we keep our focus on the positive memories with them, we relinquish our power to make changes and we often find ourselves making excuses about them and sometimes denying it is over.

Even if we are not over the person yet, by making excuses and denying it is over we are not facing the reality we need to make a new start with our full purpose and heart. I am not at all saying we should be at the stage yet where we can release them completely, just that it is hard to make progress forward if they own your memories.

I was faced with owning up to several major heartbreaks in my life by experiencing the divorce with my wife and losing my son. I came across a book, *Resilient Grieving: Finding Strength and Embracing Life After a Loss that Changes Everything*, by Lucy Hone. The reason this book touched me is because like myself losing a son, Lucy lost her daughter unexpectedly in a car accident. It is difficult when we don't get to say goodbye to ones we love.

In the middle of the darkness it is easier to not want to own the situation and slip deeper into the abyss of negativity and blame. A comment Lucy Hone made in *Resilient Grieving* grabbed my attention. She said, "This was my situation. I needed to exert whatever control I had left and do anything humanly possible to get myself back on my feet as quickly as I could." That is a huge proclamation of self-responsibility in the midst of a personal crisis. It reminded me that I needed to face my realities that had become my life. I had to accept that my son was gone and was never coming back. I also had to realize that my ex-wife wanted this divorce and there was no changing her mind.

The advantage I had in coping with the loss of my son was that my ex-wife understood exactly the feelings I was having. Knowing that placed some peace between us after Dylan died. The compassion that was lacking toward my ex-wife had returned after our son's death. I am at awe how mothers move on after a death of their children. I was devastated as a Dad, and I cannot even imagine how a mother, who carried the baby biologically and psychologically, copes with a loss of that magnitude. Even with being able to own the situation better, partially though discussions with my ex-wife, I still realized my marriage was over with her.

The goal of this chapter is to get to the point that full awareness is placed on the fact that it is over. When you are clear that it ended, then you can rebuild and start over. It is time to look forward. Your ex made the decision they did not want this any longer and now is our turn to say, "OK, I accept that." Acceptance does mean that you agree with the decision. It just means that you know this is your *current* reality and we are no longer going to make excuses for why it happened. We also can make the decision that we are not staying in something that has left us behind. This may sound harsh, but so is the reality of confronting that it is over.

In Chapter 2, we were just learning to cope with the river of dark thoughts hitting us consistently. In this chapter, we are starting to build a foundation of our own. If we are giving all of our energy to our ex we are building a foundation on quicksand.

The chapters ahead will be more positive and will focus on *you* primarily and not on the ex. First, we have to accept the reality of our situation so we are back in control. Again, this is not about being completely over them, it is about being in a place where we can build a strategy for you.

What do excuses and denial look like? If you have excuses about whether it is really over, you will have an inner dialogue about it. The dialogue can come in different forms.

Some of the excuses and stances of denial I hear

- She will be back

- He will miss me

- No other man has what I have

- We have kids together. There is no way he would be with another woman

- I am the best thing she ever had

- It isn't over. The phone will ring in no time

- She needs me

- He won't accomplish anything without me

Some of the responses stem out of anger toward the other person rejecting us. Other parts come from self-preservation and our ego trying to keep us in the game. These excuses and denial statements are all trying to serve us, but in reality, hold us back from moving ahead.

The feeling of being angry and hurt is natural. Just try not to live in that place for too long. As it is said, we are either growing or dying. This is a place of dying as long as we stay here. Not physical dying as much as mentally.

I am guilty of this when I started my comeback. I would have a couple of rum and Cokes and I would remember saying to myself, "She is about to lose the talent in the family." The statement was extremely arrogant but made me feel better in the moment. The alcohol also boosted my level of self-importance in my mind.

I was beyond angry that I was trying hard when she didn't want me anymore. Now I know I could have cut the pain quickly, and built my life for me instead of worrying about what she felt about me. It felt good to make her the fault of the divorce in my head. Then in a separate breath I was remembering all the good times we had. My mind was a mess. One second I couldn't stand her and the next I was talking about her like she was the Queen of England.

This is often the place where people look for revenge toward their ex for ruining their life. Revenge can be classified as things that are done to the other person mentally or done to them verbally. Often, we hear about people going to their ex-wife or husband's homes and vandalizing the home or their car. Another form of revenge is posting on social media or telling people negative things about the ex, even if it is opinion based.

Revenge does not serve your long-term purpose. It may feel great in the moment to get even, but always brings Karma full swing by getting you a restraining order, a trip to court for charges, or a return fight that ends ugly. It is best to realize that each effort toward revenge just hurts yourself and ability to move on.

Part of the reason we are not moving on from the relationship is because we are not considering enough of the negatives that were in play during that time. I was reading a book by Anthony Robbins titled, *Awaken the Giant Within: How to Take Immediate Control of Your Mental, Emotional, Physical and Financial Destiny!* I remember seeing the book on my shelf and I thought that awakening the giant in myself would be a terrific goal right now.

I remember a chapter in *Awaken the Giant* on the importance of questions. Tony had mentioned that questions determined the quality of our thoughts. He also noticed that we ask ourselves questions all day long to create dialogues in our heads. Tony stated, "I began to realize that thinking itself is nothing but the process of asking and answering questions."

Tony Robbin's chapter on questions sparked me to start asking myself questions about my relationship ending. I wanted to believe I had a marriage made in heaven. In reality, I saw only the positive aspects of the relationship. I wanted to end these thoughts so I reversed the questions to help me determine why the breakup was a terrific idea.

My initial question to myself was, "What is great about this divorce?" I based the list fully on emotion, so some of the answers were steep and sided with my ego. This is the initial sample list that came out of my head onto paper:

1. It offers me the chance to become all I ever wanted without limitations.

2. It gets me out of the bad energy that has been brought to the relationship for a long time.

3. No more guilt!!

4. The chance to design everything the way I want it in my life.

5. I can decorate the way I want.

6. I will have quiet nights to build a new life.

7. No more fights over superficial stuff.

8. No more house guests I don't want.

9. I can focus 100 percent of my energy on the boys.

10. I can set up the house for health and fitness versus junk food.

11. I can then have 100 percent accountability to myself and have to own it all.

12. I won't have to have opinions I did not want about all areas of life.

13. Peace: There will no fighting and screaming. I will have a chance to breathe.

14. With the quiet, I will have clarity to build my dreams and goals.

15. No more waiting on others and being impacted by others.

16. A chance to do it right compared to the lessons I learned from my parents.

17. I can cook what I feel like making each night.

18. I can have set patterns for myself and the boys.

19. The chance to be civil and let her see what she gave up.

20. The chance to open the right energy for the woman who is the right fit for me in the future.

21. No excuses. It is all on me. Find a way.

22. I can put everything on a calendar again and ensure pure effectiveness.

23. Learn new skills. Change my identity and the way I am living overnight.

24. Form some weekly rituals with the boys that will last a lifetime without interference.

25. I can remove the brakes and live life without limits.

The list can be as long as you want it for yourself. The main point was to get on the benefits of heading in your own direction versus feeling like we need to stay with the person who just let us go. It gets the mind to perceive options for your own life outside of a relationship. It gives you some items to aim for when making the future much better than the past.

There is always a light at the end of the tunnel. The list I made had me feeling much better. I started to see some positive aspects of being done with the relationship. I would not consider my relationship a negative experience in terms of being with a bad person.

My ex-wife has always been and will always be a good person, but my list allowed me to cope with her leaving our marriage. For many people, the relationship wasn't a fit but people stay anyway because they didn't want to lose the familiar.

In the book, *Intimate Relationships* by Ralph Erber and Maureen Wang-Eber, the authors stated, "We commonly assume that many of us experience sadness in the aftermath of a dissolution of a relationship, but undoubtedly some of us experience a great deal of relief when a bad relationship ends." Find the relief about your relationship ending and you will feel better in owning the outcome.

I realize that the decision that it is over makes it a prospect of faith and hope to go forward. Know the mulling over it is just a way to waste today and the number of days in front of us. So, the choice is to stay stuck where we are or we can make the decision that it is over for us so that we can move on.

We need to draw a line in the sand. Do we take a fresh new adventure and do it our way, or do we continue to hang on in the hopes that they really didn't mean to break up with us? It is a confusing time, but a vital one to be able to head our own direction instead of staying in a direction that is connected to them.

Inspiration Checkpoint

This is our path and always will be. There is no better day than today to getting on our path and making our lives meaningful to us. Follow your path and let your ex follow theirs.

One key distinction is that we need to stop seeking their approval immediately. Even if you took actions to try to prove yourself worthy in their eyes, the chances are that the actions will go unnoticed or unappreciated. That same energy can be put into your own life.

It is time to start untangling your identity from the identity that was created by both of you together. In order to live the future that we would like to live, it has to be built on our own identity and on what we want.

I know it seems like they just made a harsh decision and did not consult us until we were advised of the result. It is important to understand that they had a rough time too and feel deeply guilty in most cases about ending the relationship. There can be negative karma that they carry by making the decision that they did. It isn't always an easy decision to make, but sometimes needs to be made.

We can choose to live established habits and continue on the path we are going, and reinforce that direction with excuses and thinking the same thoughts moment-to-moment, or we can step out and own what is front of us. When reading a book by Wayne Dyer, *Excuses Begone! How to Change Lifelong, Self-Defeating Thinking Habits*, I came across a passage that had me question the story I was telling myself about the relationship being fixable. It also addressed the excuses I was making for my ex. Wayne said, "The truth, as I see it, is that everything you think, speak, or act as you've done for your entire life, when you abandon making choices, you enter the vast world of excuses" I had shut down the choices I made toward self and the excuses flowed. I started thinking about how much energy I was giving a situation that was dead.

During the time that I was researching heavily on how to get out of the pain I was experiencing, I came across an insight that truly got me thinking. It was in the form of a question, and mentions something like, "Is it really that I want her back? Or, "Am I really just upset about the rejection that I am experiencing and not doing a break up on my terms?" The questions are valid.

I could see years of problems in the relationship, but I always wanted to believe that marriage was just hard work and that the problems that I was experiencing were part of life. I didn't have a solid education in making the marriage work due to the problems between my parents.

As a matter of fact, most of us don't come into a marriage with the framework of what will constitute success in the marriage or relationship. What the question did for me is show me that it easily could have gone the other way where I was the person doing the dumping instead of being dumped. My value of staying married forever clouded my view of the true problems that existed in the relationship.

The one lesson that stands out to me the most, and fits every chapter in this book, is that we have to be able to love ourselves first. It is impossible that we are the best version of ourselves to others if we do not exercise self-care. Right now, it is extremely important that we are gentle with ourselves and we see the good sides of ourselves. It is also very important that we focus on our own self-esteem and self-image as we get ready to build a life of our choosing.

At the present moment, the familiar life that you had is stripped out from under you. I have been there. It is also a glowing opportunity to see what is right for us instead of what we've come to accept over time. I am not speaking specifically about the relationship when I mention the standards that we have allowed ourselves to live with. Before coming across Tony Robbins book, *Awaken the Giant Within*, I hadn't realized how badly that I let my standards drop to a very low level compared to the dreams and visions I had for the future. I felt I needed to do anything for the marriage but became too comfortable in terms of loosely considering my own standards and values.

In the later chapters in the book we will spend a good deal of time looking forward and seeing what the future should be about for us. I can tell you unequivocally that now is the time to decide that today is a fresh start. Today is the day to allow ourselves to stand on our feet with pride and know that something better is coming. That starts with the decision that you are done with the entire situation with your ex. I do understand if kids are involved, and exchanges of the kids are involved, but this is really about you getting on with something much more inspiring than what you are coming out of.

Your path is always your path, regardless of who you are in a relationship with. Your ex has their own path as well. The choice they made to end the relationship is something that they will need to live with in the future. Only they know if they have done what it takes to do the inner work of moving on without having issues re-occur for them in the future. Don't tap your brain with thinking about whether they made a mistake or not. It is their mistake. Have pride in yourself and decide that today is the day you will move forward.

Embracing Single Life

After almost 30 years with the same person, it was hard for me to believe that I was single again. I didn't know what to think about that because my identity was one of being in a relationship and being married for so many years. In that amount of time we learn to complete each other's sentences and know all the little quirks that come with a long-term relationship. It was like a rope that was intertwined together and takes a careful unraveling to turn one rope into two.

When my wedding ring came off, I almost felt naked on my left hand. I was used to having the ring on so often that there was a white band on my finger when the ring came off, from my tan. When I went out in public I would think about others and what their opinion was of the fact that I was older and was not wearing a wedding ring. The ring was always a source of pride in the past and showing that I had somebody who I loved and connected with. Now without it, I just simply didn't know how to perceive my life forward.

One thing that I learned in a hurry was to embrace my singlehood. The schedule was mine now. Though I had my sons every other week, the weeks in between were mine to do what I wanted to do. I could work on my new career, the one I am doing now, and think about the future a lot more often than just a hectic day-to-day stuff that I had done in my marriage. I could go out with a friend and not worry about what time I returned home.

I noticed that I started enjoying the process of the moments, from having a great tasting and smelling cup of coffee, to sitting down to watch a movie I was looking forward to. When I watched movies, I now had surround sound and was not bothering anyone else in the house by turning it up and enjoying the experience. I was having genuine and rich conversations again and knowing that I could get more out of each moment I was living. There are many things about being alone that are fantastic if we are not thinking about loneliness and about having someone else swoop in to save us emotionally. There are little treasures all around us that we will notice if we are looking for them.

Reputation with Others

Another challenge that I had with admitting that my marriage was over, was that I didn't know how to tell the story of how the divorce happened. It was inevitable that people would ask how did the marriage end. I just didn't know what to say. It was almost an embarrassment that I could not hold a relationship together of almost 30 years. It was another area that you could classify in the topic of fear and uncertainty. Again, I was held back by a simple emotion and the way I represented it in my mind.

So, the goal now, since we can't go back and erase our entire past, is to accept that it's over and go to sleep tonight knowing that it is over. It is time to move forward. We have to be willing to start over. One of the ways, as I have previously mentioned, is to ask yourself some key questions.

Below, I will provide some questions to get you started that can help you toward embracing that it is over with the ex. I realize that some people will perceive this exercise as adding a negative energy toward the person who left them. I also realize that if we are honoring and thinking positively all day long about our ex-relationship, it will be impossible to move forward with full purpose in heart into a direction that is right for us.

Questions to Help You Move On

- What is great about this breakup (or divorce), or what could be?

- Was there ever a time when you thought about breaking up the relationship yourself? Why?

- What are some qualities or beliefs of your ex that drove you crazy?

- What are some of the things that you would never do with your ex but would do now that you are out of the relationship?

- What are the differences in the relationship that you had to compromise on consistently?

- What are some of the relationships they had (family, friends) with people who drove you crazy or brought stress to your life?

The above questions will get you started. You can think of some on your own, or come up with thoughts on your own, that will tell you inside that it is good that it's over. I am not at all saying to demonize the person. I am saying that you have things that you know are more fulfilling for you that you necessarily could not do with that other person. With the relationships being such a huge compromise, there has to be some things that you feel great about now that the relationship is over.

Before leaving this chapter, it is ideal that we know the relationship is over in our heads. The memory will not be so vivid as time goes on. Forgive yourself. You did the best you could with what you had in skills and knowledge. Release your regrets and allow yourself to go forward with honor.

Remember the words of Bob Proctor and Sandra Gallagher from their book, *The Art of Living*. Bob and Sandy described, "When you react, you put the situation or the person in control of you. When you respond, you stay in control." Try to take a step back before each action and evaluate if the action is going to move you forward.

The next chapter is devoted to creating the actions that are necessary for you to take now that the relationship is over. Now we are heading in a direction that is about "I" and not "we." You are making huge strides and you will see just how incredible this will be later if you continue your momentum.

<u>Key Takeaways, Tools, and Lessons</u>

- Over time, we tend to remember the good in situations that we experience and we set aside a lot of the negative or traumatic experiences that existed. The same thing happens with a relationship, when we try to make the other person better in the relationship than they truly were. A large portion of the reason that things went so well in the relationship had to do with us being involved

- The entire goal for this chapter is to be able to get it clear in our minds that the relationship is over. This is our current reality and what we need to know to move forward

- We can't go north and south at the same time. We must pick a direction to head

- Acceptance does not constitute agreement. We don't have to like the decision they made but we do need to live with the decision that has been made

- Forget about getting revenge on the person. It is negative energy for you, and can only end badly. They must live with their own decision, and it may have been the wrong decision. But it is their path just as you have your path

- Using questions to stimulate thinking is an excellent tool. In this chapter, we are using questions to narrow to our own self-interest, and to determine what we really did not enjoy about the person we were with

- Set your mind to respond instead of react to circumstances. Take a minute before reacting and figure out a more effective way to respond before doing so

- If you do not have a reason to be around you ex right now, remove the need to contact them or get around them. By staying away, you will allow yourself time to think about you and not them

- Take time for self-care and being gentle to yourself. Making the focus on you will help the decision to break free a better possibility

Chapter 4

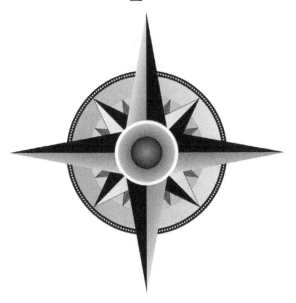

Separation:
The Reality Hits

"Acknowledging the plain truth is the first step in acceptance. It doesn't mean you have to like what's happening, simply that you acknowledge reality."

— M.J. Ryan

Now that we accepted that the decision has been made and we must progress forward, the question arises, "What is next?" The next step is to gather our thoughts quickly so that we can take the appropriate actions for self-preservation and to get on track while we build on the foundation we created in the last chapter.

There are two distinct areas that we need to take action on. One is immediate needs (today through 90 days forward). This pertains to those that must be done at this time to get on our feet. Some of these actions may include:

- Finances and having a way to live (if a concern)

- Places to live (if we are not staying in our current place). Do we need to do this with a roommate or without?

- What to do about the children or pets (if applicable)

- How to separate the material possessions

- Transportation (if needed)

- If a divorce, we will need to figure out what our exes intentions are and to see if they are willing to negotiate

- Creating a contingency plan. If the relationship is ending, but you are not physically separated yet, it is a great time to create a *Plan B*. If the separation has already happened, and you are displaced from your location of living, then there are more pressing needs to figure out like how to get a roof over your head and to have food to eat. For some people, this is not a concern, but this is very situational, based on who is going through the breakup

- Additional employment if you need ways to make ends meet.

I was fortunate enough, after all of the initial fighting with my ex-wife, to get to a place where we could file a divorce and work out arrangements for the kids and property and asset divisions. We were able to this without having to obtain attorneys. If you are going through a divorce I will nudge you, but not nag you, to appeal to your ex's human side to work things out without investing a ton of money into attorneys. By taking this approach, you can both head into your new life with more resources financially. There are situations where attorneys are necessary, or just needing them to get the paperwork filing done in the correct way. Going after each other because of hurt or ego is just a huge waste of resources.

The other area of action that we should be thinking about are the longer-term resolutions of a marriage or a breakup. If your ex files a divorce, there is usually a time gap to try to come to a better resolution with that person. This is why it is not an immediate need. This area of action includes agreements for a divorce, habits that we must take to be concerned with self-care, the well-being of our children if applicable, setting up some boundaries and standards that we will correspond with when engaged in conversations with the ex (if we must interact), how we will co-parent our children, and anything else that we can think of after the first 90 days following the breakup.

It is difficult to provide you with all of the right tools in this category, because everyone's situation is so different. The way to think about the action phase, is to realize what must be done today versus what can be done later. If it helps, at the top of the page of paper, list the question, "What are the immediate actions I must take to survive after this breakup?" Do not overthink it as stress will reduce the quality of your answers. Simply trigger yourself off of that question to start writing.

> # *Inspiration Checkpoint*
>
> The act of getting ideas out of your head and on to paper reduces the stress that comes with having to remember it all. Just know that you are investing in the future by getting action plans together, even if merely for survival.

There are no right or wrong answers, only ideas about what must be done. I know many people who use a mind map and simply write the question in the middle of a piece of paper and then start drawling lines from it with subcategories of what must be done. If you choose this method you can use some of the topics above to get started and then create some of your own.

The main concern right after a breakup is where you will live, how you will afford to live and eat, and how you will handle things with your job to keep income stable. If there are children involved, they are certainly a priority. This includes the way the conversations go around them and their and emotional well-being, and where they will spend their time. If it is a dangerous situation for the children because of safety concerns, the courts have some ways to file an injunction to get temporary custody until legal matters can be worked out. Take the time immediately to start listing your priorities of what needs to be done.

After you get a good list going, and you run out of ideas, then go back and put them in priority order as usually some of your actions are a lot more important than others. Even though you are in a time that feels like complete hell, do not procrastinate as it can make your conditions much worse.

This is a time to dig deep and find the reasons that you must get on your feet immediately. It truly helps when money is of no concern in the process, but most people do not have the luxury of having finances completely taking care of. So human needs come first, and emotional needs would come after. Human needs, as mentioned, are food, shelter, transportation, income, and the survival and well-being of your children if applicable.

After the initial needs are met, if you are in a situation where you have to see your ex, because of children or social ties, it is good to sit down and write out boundaries for that relationship. For example, I had two children under the age of 18 that I had to do exchanges with my ex-wife. At the start, seeing her and interacting with her had me walking on eggshells. I didn't know when a fight was going to erupt, which impacted the well-being of the children.

I set it up with her that we would each have the children for one full week at a time, because that would reduce the inconvenience of exchanges with her and would also reduce the chances that a fight would be occurring in front of the children. I set up my own rule that if a fight started, I would not be the one to start it, and I would immediately ask the kids to get in the car and I would tell my ex-wife that I have to leave for an appointment. I was not doing that to disregard her feelings. I was doing that to make it easier on the kids and to lessen the amount of negative emotional investment that I was putting into the situation. When I was in the relationship, the boundaries were less clear. After the relationship, I could define it any way that made it easier. It turned out to be great for my relationship with my ex-wife that we started behaving in this way.

This chapter is shorter because most of the effort will be between you and a writing pad. Just the act of sitting down and getting things out of your head and onto paper removes stress that may be occurring for you.

It also creates a written document which will help the attention in your mind to remember what must be done and actioned. Since you will be prioritizing your list, you will know what needs come first. One added step that you can do is to add a timeframe to each action, in case it must be business days when the items can be completed. Obviously, the actions that address the worst possible consequences must come first.

The prerequisite to getting moving again toward the future is to believe in yourself. It may seem overwhelming right now but I'm sure you can remember other things in your life that were difficult for you that that you amazed yourself when you conquered them. Keep in mind the words of David Schwartz who wrote the book, *The Magic of Thinking Big.* "Believing something can be done paves the way for creative solutions. Believing something can't be done is destructive thinking. That point applies to all situations, little and big," David says. Even if you don't believe in or trust yourself to plan and take actions to get necessities taken care of, there are always examples of others who have done it. Millions of people have seen the same struggles and gone on the have the lives they never thought they would live.

Remember that simplicity is always a great rule. Simplicity allows you to stay uncluttered when you need it the most right now. As mentioned prior, when stress is high and many emotions are dark, the quality of planning and thinking lowers. By having simplicity and priorities you are putting yourself in a position to make more quality decisions about what must be done, and opening up options of how they can be done.

The most difficult part of deciding how I would get on my feet after the divorce was due to the emotions and clutter combined. I turn to Brain Tracy's philosophies and books when I am in a place where priorities are not coming to me easily. In his book, *Get Smart: How to Think and Act Like the Most Successful and Highest-Paid People in Every Field,* Brian summarizes the GOSPA Thinking Model. This model has five components. In order they are, goals, objectives, strategies, priorities, and actions.

Goals: The specific, measurable, time-bounded results you are seeking to achieve.

Objectives: The short-term goals within the larger goals that must be achieved in order to reach your bigger goals.

Strategies: A brainstorming of possible ways you can achieve each of your objectives. For example, if you are trying to find a place to live, you could write your criteria for the place you are looking for and how you will make it work to lock the place in.

Priorities: The activities that are more important than other tasks in order to hit your objectives and goals. Try to combine steps in a way that you can skip some actions if others will get you to your result faster. The final result is what matters.

Actions: The activities you must take to put your strategies, objectives, and goals into reality. Again, you want these to be specific, measurable, and time-bounded.

During this time, your brain will be very busy. The good news is that your brain will be busy doing something that is productive to move you forward. It will feel more gratifying that you are progressing instead of sitting down and putting yourself in the role of a victim that cannot do anything about their situation. I will include some questions below that can trigger some answers for you during this planning and writing process. Again, every person's situation is differently so brainstorming your own list of issues can help you to create your plan.

Questions to Get You Started

How and where will I live?

Do I need to move?

Can I afford to stay here or is it a choice?

Do I need a roommate?

Can I afford it here?

How will I eat?

Am I able to do this financially?

If not, will a second job make a difference?

Are there areas I can cut expenses?

If income is very low, are their agencies that can help until I get on my feet?

Can I subsidize expenses by sharing a place or living with someone?

If Applicable:

What are the top needs of the children?

Survival (food, shelter)?

Emotionally?

Who will have the children?

Are they safe with the ex?

How can I get to work and back (if transportation is a challenge)?

Are there any ideas I am not thinking about now that can make a difference?

Once the immediate action planning is done and you are safe and established in the new or existing environment, you can spend more time thinking about the next phase of actions. There is no right or wrong timeframe, just that your immediate needs are met first.

After you are situated with housing and income, and other finances, as well as the kids, you can relax the mind. You can get on with defining what habits you will need to make a ritual each day, what you will need to do to establish yourself further in the place you're living, and how your emotional needs and those of your family will be met.

At this stage, we have figured out what we need to do in this immediate time and space, what our priorities are, and came up with some action plans to meet them. As my friend Dr. Sanjay Jain states, "Determining your priorities and figuring out your best options are great uses of your time." Sanjay's book, *Optimal Living 360: Smart Decision-Making for a Balanced Life*, offers tools to help make life a more balanced approach.

I spent some time with Sanjay last year in California and I can tell you that this man is all about balance. He has benchmarks for every area of life, from his medical practice, to the way he treats finances. Take the time to plan for a future that allows you to hold up all of the most important parts of life when you are weathering the storms that life will undoubtedly send your way.

As mentioned prior in the book, investing in pads of paper and spiral notebooks with the writing pens is a great thing to do. It will help you a lot in this section of the book, and will allow you to get your thoughts organized. Eliminate distractions and do your planning in a place that is quiet if you have that luxury. Turn off your phone and computer and focus on getting the most complete answers that you can do. I made a cup of tea or coffee in these situations and took time to breathe before starting. I smelled the coffee or tea and took in the moment.

"When your marriage falls apart, when a job that defined you is gone, when the people you'd counted on turn their backs on you, there's no question that changing the way you think about your situation is the key to improving it. I know for sure that all of our hurdles have meaning. And being open to learning from those challenges is the difference between succeeding and getting stuck."

— Oprah Winfrey

Oprah has sparked inspiration in me for years. I watch all of her Super Soul Sunday episodes and sit actively with my ears open and a notepad to catch any insights that can make a difference. Sometimes when I have thinking blocks toward the current day, I get a load of "aha" moments that fuel my thinking and spirit. I respect her work because at a time when other TV notables were spewing trash all over TV, Oprah choose a route that would help people grow and adopt a new energy. That coupled with the challenges she overcame in life to be such a role model, influenced me to tune into her vision and offerings.

Oprah authored a book in 2014 with the title, *What I know for Sure*. I immediately bought a copy. The timing of her book was against the time I was going through my divorce. In the book she mentioned, "What I know for sure is that pleasure is energy reciprocated: what you put out comes back. Your base level of pleasure is determined by how you view your whole life." That is what I needed to hear in order to take action on planning a path ahead. I realized that small moments mattered and it nudged me into creating an action plan of what I needed to accomplish immediately to get back on my feet. I knew that it was time for better moments in my life.

Figure out what today requires from you to stabilize your situation. As mentioned, stop to make a cup of tea or coffee of your favorite brand. Breathe and relax and start with a calm mind versus one that is scattered and gets in the way of the mind helping you to determine your direction.

If you have self-talk getting in the way of enjoying the small moments and keeping you from advancing, blaze the words from Robert Anthony into your mind. He stated, "Your number one priority in life is your own well-being and the expression of your awareness."

<u>Key Takeaways, Tools, and Lessons</u>

- The most important step right now is figuring out what you must do for housing, food, income, children, and transportation. All other answers came come after

- Invest in pads of paper or spiral notebooks and some pens so you have a place to make your action plans

- List ideas without over-analyzing. Just get it all down on paper. You can also use mind mapping where you write one central question in the middle of the page and just let your brain go to work on coming up with subtopics

- Make sure to prioritize your actions so that the most important items are done first. Schedule them if possible

- Simplicity is key. Keep your descriptions short when possible, and know that you have a lot to deal with so don't weigh yourself down in details

- After all of your immediate needs are met for how to live, you can start on other actions that will keep you afloat emotionally and physically

- Be sure to take care of yourself during this entire process

Part Two
Recovering

"It's when changes are big, painful, confusing, and/or disruptive of your hopes and dreams, that it's hard to see there is a process at work. Being aware of this process can help us avoid getting stuck along the way, suffering needlessly in using up precious time. For were not just being asked to adapt these days, but to do it speedily."

— M.J. Ryan

Chapter 5

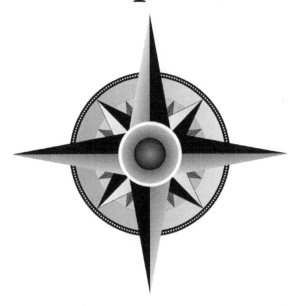

Taking Control: Enough of the Pain!

"The only thing you sometimes have control over is perspective. You don't have control over your situation. But you have a choice about how you view it."

— Chris Pine

By now it seems that we have been to rock-bottom, then started getting a foothold by knowing the relationship is over and creating some actions to move forward immediately. Now that we have the basic needs met and have a foundation built to create a new life on, the goal of this chapter is to move beyond surviving and start taking control of what will be a more rewarding future for us.

With so much turmoil, it is very difficult to see the good in ourselves and to have confidence at the level that we would like to. But it is vital right now to love ourselves and to really be flexible and gentle with ourselves because of all that we are taking on.

We are now heading into a more inspiring and feel-good section of the book as we have already paid our dues toward negative feelings that nag us. We will do more to avoid pain then we do to head toward pleasurable experiences in life. The irony is that the things we often do to lift the pain are intended to make life more pleasurable.

Now we are at the stage where the lines are blurred as the pain is still existent but is not as heart-piercing as it was prior. We have taken the transition from our ex being fully in charge, to now having our own views moving forward. This is the start of a meaningful life.

The term self-care has been mentioned a couple of times but is so vital to us becoming the best version of ourselves. It is difficult to be 100 percent present for the people we love in our lives if we are not at a place where we feel good and emotionally empowered. This comes from daily grooming, getting our bodies moving, and growing in our knowledge.

We will also take out the notepads again for this chapter and start listing everything we can think of that we would like to be doing right now. We are free to make the future whatever we would like. Some ideas include:

- Music. Making playlists that we can use for exercise, while cooking, while lifting our spirits, or just to have time that we are content with

- Fitness. It can be as simple as committing to taking a walk during lunch time or in the evening and getting the body moving. The brain functions better when oxygen is flowing through it. As you will remember from earlier in the book, changing the body also changes the mental state that we are in. Mental state changes are useful when we are trying to take control of our lives

- Entertainment. Do you like to go miniature golfing? Do you like to go golfing? Do you like to go to movies? Or just watch movies or TV shows at home? Do you enjoy going to coffee with friends? Do you enjoy diving into a great fiction or nonfiction book? Do you like your neighbors and feel like having more meaningful conversations with them? Do you want to learn to cook differently? Would you like to get out somewhere with your kids? Do you have family or friends that you would enjoy more time with? Are there some things on your list that you always said you would do and haven't done yet?

Making Home Your Home

The purpose of this phase is to connect and love yourself at the core. Do what feels good. Make your life a reflection of the meaning you want it to have. Make your home more soulful and full of purpose and meaning that attaches to where your life is heading. I was viewing a DVD about an Internet marketer named Marie Forleo. Tony Robbins, in his series, *The New Money Masters* was interviewing her as she has created a full career running an Internet business from her laptop. She was talking about how in the early days money was tight and she was living in New York in a tiny apartment. She said something that had a profound effect on me.

I always had a grand vision for my living conditions. I wanted to have a nice environment before I would invest and personalize décor and want to make my home the place that was truly mine. I set up the expectation in my mind that I would have to have bigger goals in order to set up a place that meant a lot to me.

Marie mentioned that no matter where your life is at the moment, always make your place your castle. If you have a tiny studio apartment or a large home, do all that you can to make it feel special and meaningful to you. Marie mentioned putting out flowers on her small dining room table so she had something beautiful to look at and smell. Her interview really changed my perspective.

It came time to move into my apartment after the divorce while my house was being built. One day I decided that I truly enjoyed a good cup of coffee or espresso. I made sure that my place, at that time, had an espresso maker and a Keurig. I did not buy expensive models because I had so much money invested to move forward after the divorce. And though the coffee and espresso was not the best on the planet, it was mine.

Since moving to my house after the apartment, I added a high quality Breville espresso maker, a Starbucks Verismo system for instant espresso, and the latest Keurig model that makes coffee or dispenses hot water for tea. In addition, I have purchased framed quotes, inspirational reminders, photo collages in frames for pictures of my kids and family, and painted with colors that are calming and a reflection of where I want to be in my life.

My first step was to learn how to change the energy in my home. I wanted a positive place for me and the boys to come home to every day that inspired great thoughts, great conversations, and really allowed us to be ourselves when at home. My first book about energy in the home was by Jayme Barrett and is called, *Feng Shui Your Life*.

The book was incredible in getting my thoughts to a place where I solve the true importance of making my life around meaning. It lifted me and my thinking and showed me how vital it was to focus on what is important to me. Jayme commented, "I believe that in order to change your life, you must breathe new energy into the way you think, speak, act, work, love and, of course, design your surroundings. Shifting your perceptions, attitudes, and behaviors immediately influences your actions. Your actions create your destiny."

Jayme's book gave both strategies for changing the environment while also philosophically giving alignment to the environment we are setting up. I knew that home was like a battery charger, from the energy in the home to the level of rest I was getting there. In the book, she shows how to not only organize your home, but a different way to approach life. This is exactly what I needed to hear after going through a difficult break up and starting fresh on my own.

Considering What You Want

I ask you, what are some things that you have always considered doing for your life that you just haven't found the time, energy, motivation, or will to go after? Would you like to go to school for a certain topic? Are there some books on your reading list you just haven't got around to? Are there some people that you want to spend time around and just haven't? Are there some projects that have been left undone that you need completion to? Life is yours now. Take advantage of the time to make yourself a priority.

In short, do more of what makes you happy in larger doses. Also, do less of what makes you miserable, in smaller doses. Richard Koch summed it up perfectly: "Identify the times when you are happiest and expand them as much as possible. Identify the times when you are least happy and reduce them as much as possible. To know the difference is a huge insight and one that can make more of a difference in your life than any other insight.

The Use of Power Symbols

One thing that I decided to do was to keep my mind productive and focused on the future I wanted. I didn't want the distraction of other people's dialogues. I created something I called a Power Symbol. I had taken the time to do everything I have taught you in this book so far, and I had taken time to create a future that would be everything I wanted. I have done this in stages but have made it a cornerstone of my life knowing what the next 10 and 20 years are going to look like for me.

The challenge had been to stay on track when times were difficult and not dip below the standard that I had set for myself. I asked myself what I could do as a consistent reminder to stay true North to my values and my visions for the future. I decided that as a Power Symbol to I would wear a necklace everywhere. I purchased a compass pendant. The pendant would give me a moment-to-moment reminder to stay on track. I have committed to having this power symbol in multiple places around me at all times.

You will notice a compass graphic throughout this book. The compass is present in my energy while writing this book for you, as a reminder of to keep focused on my values and direction consistently. After my marriage, I lost my compass. My girlfriend, after the divorce, found the only company online that made my compass pendant and she bought me a new necklace and pendant. It was inscribed on the back and states, "Always Know True North – SB." She understood the meaning of the compass to me. It was my constant reminder and energy for where I was heading in life.

You can choose your own power symbol. Your Power Symbol is a great way to remind yourself what is truly important. I built on my concept and expanded my compass collection. I added a brass compass in a display box. Prior to that, I received a sextant navigational tool from my grandfather when he passed away. My grandfather was the captain of the research ship called the Atlantis II.

It was the same ship that went on later to discover the Titanic. The submersible called the Alvin was deployed from the Atlantis II to get footage of the Titanic. Once again, that was the universe showing me to stay on track.

Your power symbol can be something you wear, something you look at consistently, something you hanging from the mirror of your car, a process you do in your life, or just a trigger to how you treat yourself every day.

My niece Justina loves giraffes. It brings her peace and holds meaning to her. You can pick an emotion or direction you want your power symbol to bring. The next step is choosing a symbol that makes that emotion or direction real for you.

You will notice that there is an image of a lion at the end of each chapter. Lions are fearless in approach and it is another way to remind me to always bring out the best in myself and move beyond fear to go after life.

The key right now is to build momentum towards your new life. The second piece of the equation that is important is to make sure you are focusing on you right now. Remind yourself of a positive future so you can remove the pain of a negative past. I made the decision to be self-sufficient and no longer have to rely on anyone else for anything, including my emotions. Part of building momentum means that you get to be in the driver's seat. That is the medicine you need when your life is been so hard recently.

One thing that truly helps the mind align with the future for you is to organize and clean your home the way you want it. We talked about making the home meaningful, and part of getting rid of stress and unwanted emotions is to have an environment that we can truly function in. A clean home and an organized home makes it possible.

After having so many people pass away around me in the last several years, I made the decision to get rid of anything that was not completely essential to my life from here forward. I had two sets of bicycles and gave one away and sold another. I cleaned out every box from my past and donated items to charity. I streamlined my entire house so that if anything happened to me it would be easy for my executor and my children to come in and get only what was important to them before selling off the rest.

I also modified all of my legal documents, from my will, to my living trust, to even a medical durable power of attorney and a finance durable power of attorney form. I gave copies to my executor after getting them notarized and put another set in my fireproof box. After mentioning that I had done this, many people came to me and asked if I was sick or dying. I told them that I was simply setting up my mind in case anything happened to me. This allowed me to live life at 100 percent without the worry of what I am leaving behind. It was a way to get clutter off the brain and reduce worry. I am amazed at people in their 70s and beyond who still don't have wills and directives for what will happen when their estates need to be handled. It may have something to do with the association of planning for death would jinx people into dying. The one thing that is certain is that we will die eventually. I felt it was best to not leave people my messes and organized it all to allow myself peace now. To me, getting organized after the divorce truly has put my mind at ease so I can concentrate on more inspiring things.

The one tool that I think is really important from this chapter is to take time to answer one simple question: "What can I do now that I would like to do to make my life more meaningful and fulfilling immediately?" List as many things as you can that will help you make your life happier in bigger doses and focus fully on what you do want and avoid what you do not want. The aim of this exercise is to fully put life in your control and doing the things that nobody else is telling you have to do. Make sure that everything you pick is something you want and not something that you feel you have to do.

Creation of a Life Doctrine

The late author and speaker, Jim Rohn, mentioned that it is a good idea to have a philosophy for how you will live your life. This includes the values you will live by, the standards you will live by, the boundaries you have set for your life, and principles that you will live by.

I took the time to create something that I call my *Life Doctrine*. Merriam-Webster defines a doctrine as, "A principle or position or the body of principles in a branch of knowledge or system of belief." My Life Compass fulfills the goals of a life philosophy and holds a bird's eye view of what is important to me in life and extends to all of my goals and timelines, my beliefs, what I want my life to be about in every area, and even includes quotes that inspire me.

My document is over 50 pages of all things that help me stay focused on the meaning of my life. I typed it up, numbered the pages, and placed the sheets into sheet protectors. I inserted the pages into a half inch three ring display binder. I added a custom cover that simply says Life Doctrine and has a picture that is a collage of everything important to me including my children. I am not saying you need to go that far to define your life, but know what's important to you. Have a way to remind yourself of what is important to you.

By having a Life Doctrine, I have something I carry with me everywhere I go that is a source I can turn to remind myself where I am going and what to focus on now. This focus keeps me from worrying about the past and defines what I must do in the present time to honor my own wishes. When I find a quote in a magazine or online, I will cut it out and print it and put it inside one of the inside covers of my binder. It has helped me centralize really good energy for when I need it.

The idea originally came to me when I was completing one of my degrees at Regis University in Denver, Colorado. Regis is a Jesuit university. I was not Catholic, but the university was a great institution and I ended up getting my first two degrees there. Part of the curriculum there was to take classes that study major religions from around the world. I noticed that I had a tendency to lean toward eastern philosophies. I was sparked to create a living document for myself that would be based on my own ideal life, and include just the most fitting qualities from a variety of religions. It was not a religious document, more focused on how I wanted to live my life.

There are no rules for how you handle your current reality and future. Remember, this can be a strategy, a game, or simply a pattern of thought you create to get yourself to greener pastures. You can build on some kind of philosophy or working document for yourself that makes sense. Some people prefer journals and others purchase reminders like art, quotes, or other items that remind them of where they are heading.

Be careful to not let habitual thinking get in your way of designing you new life. Just because habits have been formed doesn't imply that you cannot create a new way of approaching and living life. The Maxwell Maltz Foundation with Bobbi Sommer updated the classic book, *Psycho-Cybernetics* with the *New Psycho-Cybernetics*. In this book the authors stated, "Anything that has been learned can be reevaluated and challenged. Anything that has been challenged can be relearned with new data to replace the old." Just get the mind out of the way and let new thoughts and inspirations magnetize your mind. You are in control and anything that gets in your way can be easily pushed aside to make room for new growth.

Inspiration Checkpoint

Make sure to have a reminder of where you are heading so you stay on track to what is important to you. This can be a Power Symbol or a Life Philosophy in the form of a document. It is all about a life of meaning from today forward.

"The truth is that life will break us and burn us at some point on the journey. This is not pessimistic or cynical but descriptive of the geography of being alive. It is part of how we are transformed by the journey."

— Mark Nepo

From the book, *Seven Thousand Ways to Listen*

Key Takeaways, Tools, and Lessons

- The goal is to create momentum of moving your life forward. The two components are that you must focus on you, and you must do things that you enjoy

- Self-love and self-connection at the core is vital right now. Even if you do not feel like a confident or worthwhile person, act like you are. We must start with ourselves before being able to effectively interact with others

- Do what makes you happy in larger doses

- Do not do what makes you miserable, and it should be in very little doses

- Choose a power symbol that will remind you of where you are heading from here. It can be a piece of jewelry, a picture, a process you do, or any other item

- One way to feel productive and growing forward is to completely clean and organize your environment at home. You could do the same for work, but just make sure that you have less clutter in your mind

- Take time to answer one simple question: "What can I do now that I would like to do to make my life more meaningful and fulfilling immediately?"

- Create a philosophy for how you will live your life. This includes the values you will live by, the standards you will hold yourself to, the boundaries you have set for your life, and principles that will guide you

- Create a notebook or binder that is a place for you to collect good energy items to add to the previously mentioned philosophy. You can name your document. Mine is called my Life Doctrine

Chapter 6

Adapting: New Habits and Philosophy

"Motivation is what gets you started.
Habit is what keeps you going."

— Jim Rohn

The most difficult part of setting standards and ideals for ourselves is staying on track. Up to this point, we have focused on overcoming the darkest of emotions. We have made a decision that the relationship is over in our minds. We have created action lists so that we can put our new life on track. After getting established and meeting our immediate needs, we have created some actions that will make life meaningful and give us momentum of taking control of our new lives.

Now comes the phase where regression can set in if we are not careful to remind ourselves consistently of where we are heading. If you took the time to do the exercises in the last chapter, you will be way ahead when it comes to tougher situations where we could relapse.

The fact is that life throws curves at us consistently. Our brains rely on filters that have been created to simplify life. These filters exist so that we don't have to deal with the task of sorting out hundreds of thousands of thoughts a day. With that said, the brain is extremely habitual in how it handles incoming thoughts and classifies them. This is why we must be extremely careful to stay conscious and have awareness of where we are heading now.

The temptation could strike to pick up the phone and call your ex, even when you think that you got control of everything. This is not a good idea, just as it wasn't a good idea before, but will be less likely if you have truly committed to a life of your own and the meaning you want to have.

You also may be faced with tough situations if your ex met another guy or woman and it doesn't work out for them. There is a chance that they suddenly want you to come back after doing a comparison with his/her new partner. It may seem great in concept that they are begging for your attention now, but keep in mind that nothing different was done and it could lead to the same result all over again and you could waste days weeks months or even years crumbling in the same relationship over again. There is a reason that it is called *moving on.*

Take the time to balance between silence and sound. Take time to visualize the future and your mind the way that you see it ideally. Take the time to sit quietly in your own thoughts, whether in meditation or simply in relaxation, and cut all of the noise. At other times, you may want the noise. It could be in the form of music, conversations with other people, or as simple as reading emails.

It is important to give yourself a gap and think about new responses that are not conditioned ones. There is an excellent book written by M.J. Ryan. In her book, *How to Survive Change...You Didn't Ask For*, M.J. explains, "When adapting to change, we need to come up with the thoughts and solutions that are different from the ones we've used in the past. Otherwise we will just be responding in habitual ways that may not serve us now." This can require creative thinking to come up with solutions that will help keep us on track that are not based on the same conditioned ways we responded in the past.

I remember back to when I was responding to my ex like a conditioned monkey that reaches for a banana and climbs the tree the same way every time. It seemed like I had a response, and not a productive one, to every emotion she expressed and every conversation that she had brought up. Since I didn't change my approach, the relationship never got better. I was living on emotion and never taking time to step out and be creative in the way I approached our relationship.

I had to have the awareness of what situations were causing the unproductive responses and figure out a way to either deal with them in a better way, or eliminate them completely. I noticed that I was having trouble getting my unproductive self-talk out of the way.

Changing the Inner Dialogue to Condition New Responses and Behaviors

Throughout the book I have been mentioning the power of questions to bring out better responses and solutions. I first used questions to change my inner dialogue. After re-visiting *Awaken the Giant Within: How to Take Immediate Control of Your Mental, Emotional, Physical and Financial Destiny*, from Tony Robbins, and starting to look at the quality of the questions I was asking, I was able to design better questions to begin using. The full goal was to condition new possibilities for how I would approach both the divorce and the new rituals I needed to follow to get life moving again.

We are constantly evaluating our lives in our heads. Since the process is largely subconscious, below our conscious awareness, we don't realize that all we are doing is using questions internally to make our evaluations. The challenge is that we often use questions that prompt negative or low-quality answers.

An example of a negative question that people may ask themselves is, "Why do women/men always leave me?" Your brain will search files, especially ones of self-image and self-esteem issues, and come up with crappy answers. Some answers might be, "Because you are needy" or "Because you never workout" or even worse, "Because you are difficult to love." The answers are not exactly going to make you feel good about yourself.

Instead if you posed the question, like we answered earlier, to be "What is great about this breakup?" you will find your answers to much less self-victimizing and more powerful in meaning.

If you are trying to brainstorm solutions about a problem within the breakup, it is good to start with the words, "how can I ____?" I learned from Tony Robbins and even go a step further and ask a question like, "How can I get back on my feet quickly and enjoy every minute of the process?" Not only am I generating solutions by asking a question like this, but I am also prompting answers that will bring me more fun and meaning at the same time.

So many areas can be changed in quality by just creating questions in a way that quality answers will follow. If you change the meaning of why the breakup happened, you will not add suffering to your life. If you change the question about how to come up with solutions for each area, again you will see the quality of life change. Think of all of the areas that are bringing you anxiety, suffering, fear, and dread and make a list of each of these areas. Take one at a time and list "how to" questions under each that will generate a new set of solutions.

I created empowering questions for both my divorce and with how to overcome the loss of my son. I first sat down and documented every situation, statement my ex repetitively said to me that equaled pain in my mind, and what self-talk was getting in my way, and listed those as trigger situations.

I also looked at what triggered me emotionally in a negative way about my son's death. I then made a list of questions, like the ones I shared, and generated answers I could use whenever those situations came up. I noticed that I started feeling better, and even euphoric much more often due to the solutions I had generated.

New questions opened up a magical world for me because I used it in areas related to financial options, making my house an energy haven and a true home, and even in how I would treat my kids when they came over. I didn't ask, "What can I do when Devon is at my house for the week?" Instead I asked, "How can I make it a magical experience and one he will remember when he comes over next week? Then the answers flowed.

The important thing was to pause long enough that I could condition in my questions and answers more often until they were habits. The daily experience of my life changed dramatically in weeks. Before, I had dealt with the pain for months and now I had a system to break free. As Tony Robbins said in *Awaken the Giant*, "Quality questions create a quality life."

Can a better quality question actually mend a workable relationship with the ex if you have a requirement to see them? Yes, of course it can. I even made up questions that would generate better answers about how the exchanges of the kids would be with my ex, and we started bonding more around the kids versus having fights.

Some of the other benefits of questions are that they are a complete focus change tool. You can go from sitting in problems and worries to being excited about tackling challenges in a short amount of time. We talked about this earlier when discussing how to change our mental states of mind quickly. The two options were changing focus, or getting the body moving. Questions are an effective way of changing focus in a hurry. With a change in focus we can also change the meaning of an experience. When the meaning changes so do the actions or responses.

Another benefit of effective question asking is that it can help you skip steps to get to solutions. If you already know what you are trying to achieve in a situation, the way questions are asked can generate a solution that may eliminate another five or more action steps.

Our brains are used to taking a sensory-stimuli, (like something that is said, witnessed, or experienced), and having a conditioned way of dealing with it. Our brains can handle only a few thoughts at a time consciously, so we store all of our memories in file cabinets and draw from them when a situation calls for an answer. We then have a set course of action based on the meaning we stored in these file cabinets. Because of our subconscious mind storing these memories in the way we can simplify meaning and experiences, we can simplify life as we don't have to think as hard. Ultimately this process can reduce the quality of our thoughts and actions, and creates labels that are often not true for a situation. By using quality questions to evaluate situations, we can automatically delete unhelpful or invalid answers and instead generate powerful solutions.

If we change the way we think by asking better questions, we also change the way we feel, since feelings come after a thought. The feelings and meaning of the thoughts we generate lead to a certain course of action. We are not getting what is real, we are getting our interpretation of what is real. Question creation is a powerful skill to master because our entire lives will be spent in moment-to-moment evaluations of what is happening and what it means to us.

Questions can also position us to scrutinize negative beliefs in our minds. If you have a negative belief that holds you back in a certain area, a quality question can give you a better answer. For example, if you feel like you will never move forward after a relationship because you have the belief you are unattractive, you can just ask yourself the question, "What is attractive about me that people really tend to tune into?"

I used to have a complex about this because of physical qualities that I had that were contained in the punchlines of people's jokes growing up. I had a larger than normal nose and I did not get braces at an earlier age like a lot of other kids. Comment after comment conditioned me to adopt the label, "I am not attractive." It worsened when I started getting hair loss. After a few accidents and a terrible diet, I added some weight gain to the mix. When I was fresh out of my marriage I really focused on how my looks were not up to par and I crushed myself with judgment. After changing my questions, I determined that my largest qualities of attractiveness had nothing to do with my body, but instead was my quick-witted humor, ability to carry an in-depth conversation, and to be pragmatic at extensive level.

After changing my question to generate answers about my attractiveness, a joint friend set me up on a date with a gorgeous woman with huge talent. I no longer focused on what was holding me back, but instead on my strengths. We all the ability to do this.

In addition to questions to counteract negative situations and people you encounter, also do the same for unproductive and limited beliefs that are holding you back, like my previous example.

I really enjoyed a book from Noah St. John called *The Book of Afformations: Discovering the Missing Piece to Abundant Health, Wealth, Love, and Happiness*. Yes, "Afformations" is spelled correctly in his context. Noah stated that "If you want to get different results in your life, you'll have to let go of certain things you've been thinking, saying, and doing that no longer serve you. And you must be willing to truthfully examine your assumptions about life and change your behaviors accordingly."

Noah St. John gave a different way to structure questions in the book. The way he structured the questions was done in a way that the answers would be an affirmation that a result was already reached. For example, some questions he asked was, why am I worry free? Why do I enjoy a full night sleep? Why do all my friends love me? Why do I love me? Noah states, "Afformations are a specific form of empowering question that start with the word why. When you ask questions that assume that what you want is already true, you will activate the part of your brain that will seek to make it so. And that is what will unleash your hidden power to take action and change your life."

I suggest you pick up a copy of Noah's book because it gives hundreds of sample questions you can use to customize specific answers for yourself. It is a simple reading and can get your mind spinning about the possibilities that come when we ask the right questions.

Inventory What is Going Well for You

Take time to figure out what has been going extremely well for you currently and focus on those thoughts and feelings behind the progress you are making. Reinforce all that is going well now. Tell yourself that you have the confidence that has encouraged you to move beyond negative circumstances. You have the power to remove the identity of a person who no longer serves you in your life.

By having a list of all that is going well for you, the focus gets off of poverty, heartbreak, and what is missing and allows you to stay engaged with what is working. It makes a huge difference to where your energy goes. I'm sure you don't like feeling bad. If you take a piece of paper and divide it into two columns, write all that is going badly on the left side and everything that is going right or could be going right on the right side. Cross out or tear off the left side of the page.

I had a burning ceremony one night. I wrote down all of my negative thoughts, resentments, and negative beliefs and went behind my house where I had a chimenea. I released it all that night by burning the pages and decided I would focus on my list of the positive aspects of life that were in my inspiration notebooks and on my list of what was going well. Did it go perfectly? Not always, but my mind was on what was working for me instead of the deep hole the negative items I was focused on prior.

Schedule What YOU Would Like to Do

Take the time to schedule important activities in your life, and priorities that you had listed prior that you had not been able to get to in your past life. What gets scheduled gets done.

The key is to continue making progress so that you feel psychologically that you are on track to a better life. Expand on the list of activities that you made prior that will help you feel good in life. Make sure to say no to things that do not seem to your intuition to be fulfilling.

Obviously, there will be dips in your emotions. At other moments you will experience the "highs." Stack the deck in your favor whenever possible by always be focusing on where you are going and add the activities that will ensure you are doing more of what you love.

If you have not by now, ensure that you remove any reminders of your past relationship. Removing reminders of your ex will make it easier to stay on track with your new life. Remove pictures, gifts that they had bought you if it reminds you of them, any joint purchases that hold meaning of the past relationship, and anything that pulls you off the focus that this is your life from here forward.

When the mind is cluttered with dark emotions, it is very difficult to hear our inner voices. You could call your inner voices your intuition or inspirational nudges. When your mind is quiet enough you will be given direction from the universe in the best way to proceed for you. It starts with having the intention of the life you want and creating that intention into a purpose for where you are heading.

The same core principles seem to come out of most of the books that I have encountered regarding psychology and self-growth. The universal advice is to figure out a life purpose, goals for the future, action steps to get the goals, and visualizing the goals in advance. I do not disagree that clarity is a vital if we want to move a certain direction. I also agree that it is a good practice to know all the main reasons that we want to head the direction that we are heading.

The one addition that I would make to this common advice is to really consider everything from our unique preferences and path in life. It is often difficult to shut off all the external chatter of everyone telling you what you should be doing and what is good for you. This can get in the way of you going a direction that fits you like a comfortable pair of shoes.

Prior to getting a hold of my new life, and living on my terms, the day was often left to chance. I found myself filling the time by hosting friends over to my home more nights than not. Though I enjoyed the social interaction, I was finding that my son was left to do activities in the home without me. I was neglecting my time with him. My intuition was telling me I needed more time with my kids, and instead I was having people over all the time to fill the void of social conversation. I knew inside that this was the wrong move for me to make in this new life that I chose for myself.

Tim Ferriss has numerous excellent Podcasts you can listen to for free. In one of the Podcasts I was listening to, he was interviewing a man named Derek Severs. Derek had mentioned that in order to preserve his time for what was really important, he used a formula called the, "Hell Yes Formula." In short, the main point of this formula was to evaluate every invitation or use of time by asking the question, "Do I really want to do this?" If your answer is *hell yes*, then do that activity. If your answer comes back with anything but a *hell yes*, the answer is no. I looked at my objectives, standards, goals and priorities, and had them in front of me at all times. If I did not have a *hell yes* to pursue an activity, I kept the time open to do what I had dictated as important to myself.

The opposite effect can take place if we are saying no just to say no. Please make sure that you don't put yourself in a place of isolation just because nothing is good enough. It is still good to have the right social interactions. Having some of your goals focused on getting out of a set environment, can also bring fulfillment. Isolation tends to bring set patterns and reignite negative emotions that you have worked so hard to get rid of. The point is to be proactive toward where you are going, and make the most time for activities and interactions that head toward that end.

Take time to celebrate even the smallest of advances forward. It is really easy to set up expectations in your mind of how things need to be in your life. One of the largest disappointments that takes place for you will be when your reality is not matching up to the expectations in your mind. It is wise to expand your rules to make it easier to be happy and stress-free. If that doesn't happen we usually have a narrower expectation of what needs to happen for us to be happy. When that is the case, it is easier to relapse into depressing thoughts and isolation. Since this is what we are trying to avoid, find ways to make happiness and peace easier.

I would like to return to the concept of being 100 percent present in any situation we find ourselves in. I was reading a book with the title, *The Power of Now: A Guide to Spiritual Enlightenment* by Eckhart Tolle. After four different people had suggested the book, I decided to purchase it. One major concept that held value for me was to understand that we are not our minds. We have our minds but we are not our minds. Eckhart stated, "Make it a habit to ask yourself: what's going on inside of me at this moment? That question will point you in the right direction. But don't analyze, just watch. Focus your attention within. Feel the energy of the emotion." The key is to be more of an observer than reacting to every thought or emotion.

With having more presence in each moment of our lives, we are in a better spot to react positively to what is going on around us. When we are present, we can notice shifts in our thinking and emotions that may not serve us as positively as we would need right now. It is easy to fall into old conditioned patterns if we do not have full awareness now. In Chapter 8 on thriving in life, a section exists to teach being more present in life.

"We all live three lives: public, private, and secret. The secret life is where your heart is, where your real motives are - the ultimate desires of your life. It is also the source of primary greatness. If you have the courage to explore your secret life, you can honestly question your deepest motivations."

Stephen R. Covey

We often consider both our public and private lives, but do not put a lot of thought into our secret lives. It is my experience that our secret lives serve as leverage to put us on a new path and to make it more difficult to knock us off of that path. This is the perfect time frame for you to spend more time in your secret life and less attention on your public and private life. The secret life exists in your core being.

So how do we keep our new momentum going, and spend less time on thinking about our past relationship and hurts? The best trick I have found is to throw myself into the excitement, challenge, and adventure of my new life and believing this was the right direction for me. When we are enjoying our lives, alcohol or negative addictions tend to not be needed any longer.

After all the inner work that I did, I expanded my beliefs about what was possible for the future. Some of those beliefs were just dormant and in me from even before the time I got involved in my past relationship. After designing a future that was exciting for me, to live here forward, I also wrote down all of the beliefs that I would need to possess in order to make my defined future possible.

I then visited my list of beliefs and wrote down experiences that I had in my past that proved each belief to be true for me. I first listed successes for each belief to prove to my mind that the beliefs were already real. I built up each belief to be even stronger in my mind to use from there forward. It raised my curiosity about how belief could be embedded at the deepest level possible in our biology.

I picked up the book, *The Biology of Belief: Unleashing the Power of Consciousness, Matter and Miracles* by Bruce H. Lipton, Ph.D. Bruce said, "I was exhilarated by the new realization that I could change the character of my life by changing my beliefs. I was instantly energized because I realize that there was a science-based path that would take me from my job as a perennial "victim" to my new position as "co-creator" of my destiny."

Bruce is an expert on cells in the body and has studied the impact that environment and belief have on our cells. Environment and belief are strong enough to change human genetics in our bodies.

Beliefs filter the way we see the world as our reality. If we see that all things are possible in life now, we will live a more expanded future. If we believe that the past brought the only joy, that is a choice in reality as well.

Inspiration Checkpoint

After designing a life full of meaning and purpose for yourself, list all the beliefs you will need to have in order to make this new life possible.

In her book, *Pathways to the Possible: Transforming Our Relationship with Ourselves, Each Other, and the World*, Rosamund Stone-Zander stated, "Reality is ultimately a belief system, no matter how sure we are that the way we see things is the way that they really are. Our own reality is like a Geiger counter, beeping frantically as we bump into ideas and claims that violate it. But let's stretch our minds a little, let's widen the frame of what we consider possible." The previous quote expands us to the place of understanding that we get what we believe in our lives and anything against our beliefs is often scorned by us.

Woven through the chapters of this book, I have discussed areas where I applied gratitude in my life as a way to get off of negative focuses. If you haven't already done it, it is a wonderful feeling creating a full gratitude list. I placed my gratitude list inside my Life Compass notebook. I review it often when I am not on top of the world or when I feel myself slipping into some of the old thoughts or patterns.

Living with gratitude has several advantages:

1. It is impossible to hold a negative thought when you are in a place of gratitude.

2. It gets us to see what is good about our life instead of what is not working.

---

3. It opens up energy into a positive vibration, which leads to loving and gentle thoughts.

4. It reminds us that even if times are rough we have a lot of good things working in our favor.

5. It allows the universe to match our energy and give us more of what we are grateful for.

Gratitude allows us to tap into an abundant universe full of energy. This infinite energy allows us to tune into any life we want. By finding what we are grateful for, we attract more of the same into form. Gratitude equals feeling good. Feeling good is a must at this time.

Self-Care: Diving into the Art of You

We discussed in the last chapter some ideas of how to be more present in our lives emotionally. Now that we are conditioning in new philosophies and habits, self-care is a cornerstone in ensuring that we don't backtrack to old patterns and behaviors.

Take the time to nurture yourself, especially now that you've created momentum into your future. I remember when I had finally broken free from the incessant need to be around my ex and thinking about her all the time. I had created list of what my ideal life meant and had filled my days with more of the things I wanted to do in my life instead of worrying about what anyone else thought.

For many years prior, I had gone to Hawaii on business, and sometimes after leaving Oahu I would head to Maui for a few nights before going back to Denver. I was so entirely relaxed, the stress would melt off, and it felt great not wearing any shoes and having the ocean breezes and water wash over me. What I really enjoyed was hours of swimming in the waves and letting the currents shift me in different directions and feeling the sun on my face. Sometimes, four hours would go by, and I was still in the water without coming out. When I was finally done swimming, I would drink a bottle of water, and head back to the hotel.

Once at the hotel, I would treat myself to a long shower or a soaking tub experience. I was so relaxed and was breathing more deeply again. I would contrast that to coming back to Denver where I would put on a suit, always have socks on, and having the confines of wearing shoes.

What I realized was that Hawaii is a mindset in my head in addition to a real experience. I determined I could make any environment a tranquil spa versus an inhibitor to my life. In Colorado, I could have the experience of watching the snow fall outside my window, while having hot cup of tea or coffee in hand with a throw blanket over me and my favorite pajamas and slippers on. Different environment, same sense of relaxation.

The focus on moment-to-moment relaxation has been a huge focus of mine since the divorce. I have searched for additional ways to nurture myself. Sometimes I will take a hot shower at night, right prior to bedtime, put on comfortable lounge wear, and pick up an inspirational book and read in bed until I feel tired. I will be tired but inspired. I keep a writing pad and pen on my night table in case any great ideas come to me during the night.

I have opened my mind to a different world where I care more about how I feel and not how others feel I should live. Take the time to feel great and put yourself in a state of inspiration. It pays many times over. It also reminds you that everything is going to be just terrific.

One instrumental insight that I have had over time was that I can always return to fulfilling states in a hurry. From the darkest and most painful of days quickly transition to energy-driven and fulfilling days. The purpose of this chapter has been to get you to a place where the lows are shorter and the highs are extended and positive. Taking control is now needed for fulfillment.

Since experiencing the huge difference raising my energy could do for my mind and body, I have placed a focus on consistency in experiencing the increased energy. As you can tell from my writing, books are a very large piece of my life and have brought me so many ideas to create new ideas and get past challenges I have encountered.

When I stopped traveling during my time of being self-employed, I switched to a Fortune 200 company on the management team there. I was home more often for family but I was not in an environment that stirred my soul at a larger level. I forced myself to numb my creative mind before heading into work. I placed all of my emphasis at work into the people side of the business and developing people into leaders. The company I worked for managed from the top down and this did not fit my style of being creative in approach.

Books played a huge role in trying to find ways to inspire myself and others. One book that changed my views about energy and the impact on business and life is called, *Quantum Success: The Astounding Science of Wealth and Happiness.* This book by Sandra Ann Taylor reminded me to place my focus back onto to energy generation. One quote from her was enough to tune me in to the importance of energy. She said, "It's what you do with your consciousness and energy that determines all the outcomes that you experience. This truth and its realization will change your life." She went on to say, "The world exist in a constant state of flux were even a small shift of energy can create an immediate and far-reaching change in reality." After this truth hit me I knew I would need to head a new direction in life that included using my energy for a better world for me and others.

Trust in a different level of energy to get you to a higher level of living right now. Be aware of the standards that you have established for yourself and the rules that you have chosen to live by. Reevaluate them and ensure that they are fully matching who you are as a person.

Trust the actions and thoughts that you have created about making your life and inspiring journey from here. Move forward knowing that the breakup, like anything else, is just lessons from the past. You now have a new chance to do it bigger and better, or differently and better, and make your life a masterpiece that revolves around you, and the meaning that makes it all worthwhile.

Be sure to take care of yourself during this time of change. Think of ways that you can enjoy the moments of your life more. In the thriving section later in the book, I will be outlining the concept of mindfulness, which can assist you in making the most of the moments you are in.

Key Takeaways, Tools, and Lessons

- Staying on track consistently is the most difficult part at this stage. Know that you will have brief times where old patterns and thoughts sneak in. Just get refocused as quickly as possible

- Relapses happen. Just be sure to have gratitude lists and action lists that you can immediately use to get back on track. Don't beat yourself up over slipping now and then

- The brain is built to filter hundreds of thousands of thoughts each day. Understand that it will sometimes return you to places that are conditioned and not productive

- Create a balance between silence and noise. This will give balance to you and give time for inner reflection and well as activity

- Take time to figure out, and reflect on, what has been going right for you. Pat yourself on the back about the progress

- Place any important activities on a schedule and calendar

- Remember the "Hell Yes Formula" to open up your schedule for what is important. If you can't say "Hell Yes" to an activity, keep the time open for what really matters to you

- Engage yourself emotionally to be 100 percent present in your life now. This will allow you to avoid back steps as they happen and lets you get tuned back in

- Spend more time in your "Secret Life" which is the deepest part of yourself where true motivation originates

- Beliefs have the power to modify the cells and change genes. Make a list of all of the beliefs you must have to move forward with an inspiring life. Find reasons that you can list of why you know these beliefs are true for you

- Take the time to write out a full gratitude list of what you are lucky enough to have in life and review the list often. It is impossible to have dark thoughts and be grateful at the same time

- Self-care is a central focus now. Think of ways, in your current environment to find peace and relaxation

- The full focus now is to make lows shorter and make highs more extended

Part Three
Rebuilding

"Keeping your eye on the future is essential for making the most of today. You need to acknowledge where you are, but you also need to see clearly where you were going. What do you want in each of the major categories of your life? What would they look like in their ideal state?"

— Michael Hyatt and Daniel Harkavy

Authors of "Living Forward"

Chapter 7

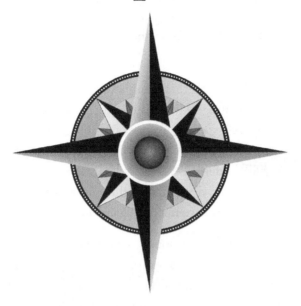

Releasing: Letting Go

"By surrendering I've become healthier, braver, more
intuitive, more flowing and fun, younger, more untamed,
and more spiritually pliant. I've shed layers of fear and
limitations that kept me locked in a life that was no longer
large enough for me."

— Judith Orloff. M.D.

There are only two directions to take after being abandoned in a relationship. One option is to pursue the other person hoping that they did not really want to break off the relationship. This can often be considered denial and holds you back from getting a positive life going for yourself. This is a situation you cannot control and can lead to problems.

The second choice is that you can surrender and trust that something more meaningful is coming for you. This allows you to prioritize your energy expenditure for only things that create a life on your terms. A lot of energy gets tied into hoping the phone will ring and everything will suddenly be healed. That same energy can be spent deciding how it will be different in the future without then ex to distort your thinking. You are making decisions fully for yourself now.

One of the common questions that I get, is "How do I let a person go when I have loved them for 20 years?" Or, "How do I stop loving a person after so many years?" My most common answer is, there is no choice but to let them go because they have they let you go. That requires a great deal of faith in your future and great deal of surrender.

If you had respect for that person or still have respect for that person, it is best to honor his or her wishes. If you spend a lot of time and energy in contacting the person it is adding to the pressure on them, and puts you in the place where you won't receive reciprocal love and respect. You will feel increased rejection and frustration that the feelings you have for them are not being returned. There is nothing worse than love that is not reciprocated.

The only two things you need in order to surrender are: faith that life will work in your behalf, and hope that life will turn out more meaningful than before this breakup. By having faith and hope, quality solutions are more easily generated to draw from.

It truly helps move you forward if you have done the work of creating a new direction for yourself, which this book helps with. It is difficult to look back when you are focused on the present and the future. It also helps to have a good support network for when you need it. Having a positive support network of friends and family can serve when you are on a path of attachment to your old partner.

We discussed setting up an environment only for you where you remove pictures and other reminders of the person so that you are not consistently triggered back into negative emotions. You may want to rid of anything that has emotional attachment to the other person. One common concern is getting rid of a wedding ring or even gifts that you received when getting married.

If you are keeping the same house, you may consider redecorating or even changing configurations of furniture and personal items to be different than before. If you have reminders that you do not want to dispose of, feel free to put them in a box out in the garage or the back of a closet. Try to minimize exposure to the items.

I had a double dose of surrender I had to own. Not only did my wife leave me, but I also had to get over the loss of my son Dylan. In both scenarios, I noticed that the most difficult part was the consistent triggers that would set me off emotionally. These triggers I had about Dylan were completely different, though some were interwoven with ones from the past marriage.

When Dylan came to my house we played darts so often that I decided to purchase him his own special set of darts to keep at my house. I leave his darts inside the cabinet now that he is gone and my younger son has chosen to take them over. It was a difficult trigger at the beginning when I would see the darts because of remembering Dylan smiling and throwing his darts. It was an experience we shared together. I remembered how we challenged each other and how it opened a door to communicate more with him while playing.

It is often the same triggers as we see from ex-intimate relationships. If you figure out what triggers are related to the unproductive responses, and think of ways to handle them when they come up, the ability to release the reaction to each quickly happens.

Letting go of a relationship after loving a person is not easy. Since we did not make the choice about ending the relationship, we don't have the luxury to think in advance how the separation will go. This is where the faith and hope come into play.

There may be fears standing in the way still of releasing a person and surrendering. By disconnecting a person from our lives emotionally, we may feel that the rejection in our heads is validated now because we have to acknowledge an ending took place.

"When a person or people in your present life trigger unwanted feelings in you, first view those feelings as memories and then intensify them. You will see that the story in which you have that person encased will probably have something to do with wanting approval or safety, or power, or desiring more closeness. Peel those stories off like wallpaper in your mind until you reveal the person in front of you as he truly is."

— Rosamund Stone-Zander

We may feel hits to our self-esteem and know that we have reality to deal with when the relationship is no longer in the way. There are painful feelings that will be attached to the release of the person, but there will also be a freedom that comes with knowing that we are no longer tied to them. In past chapters, we considered some of the positive aspects of the relationship ending. Turn to those reminders when times are difficult.

Just as when we lose somebody to death, the same grieving feelings come with losing somebody to a loss of love. The difference is when we lose someone to death, they are no longer here on a physical plane with us and sometimes it is easier to release a person since they are not constantly in the picture around us.

If we have children with another person, there is a constant reminder of the past relationship. We also will have ties to the in-laws, like grandparents, who want to visit the kids. We may have a joint business together with someone who was intimate with us. There could also be joint pet sharing with our ex. These situations are best handled with boundaries and limited timelines for verbal exchanges. Especially be careful if the disconnect is not complete between you. Having intimate relations can cause an emotional bond that is bound to end badly.

When there are no ties to the ex-partner, the commitment to releasing the relationship can be faster and easier. I am not stating that it is easier emotionally, only that there are less reasons (if at all) that you need to see the other person.

There can be times when you have been involved with you ex's family for years. Suddenly your past partner expects that you will just stop talking to her or his family immediately when the relationship is over. I know this can be difficult, especially if you ended on very escalated terms.

I remember when the times were still tense between me and my ex-wife and the discussions came up about family. I had already made the decision that I was not going to try to inhibit her from seeing my family or talking to them. They had been in her life for almost 30 years, like I was involved in her family. My ex-wife is a really good person and there was no reason I would keep her away from my family.

My only stipulation about her seeing my family was that our relationship was not discussed with them as a topic when they met up. Even though I had released my ex-wife emotionally, I did not believe that she was a bad person or deserved not to have my family in her life. When my family asked me if it's okay to talk to her, I encouraged them to but mentioned the same stipulations as above.

There are several levels of letting go. The first is being able to function on your own without feeling the need to constantly interact with your ex-partner. Gretchen Rubin, in the Oprah endorsed book, *Better Than Before: What I Learned About Making and Breaking Habits – To Sleep More, Quit Sugar, Procrastinate Less, and Generally Build a Happier Life*, Gretchen illuminates starting fresh. She mentioned, "Any beginning is a time of special power for habit creation, and at certain times we experience a clean slate, in which circumstances change in a way that makes a fresh start possible." Knowing if we let go and accept the end of the past relationship, we set up the conditions for a fresh start.

Another measure of being able to let go is accepting that we will not get back together with the ex. Part of this surrendering process is also to discontinue trying to please them in any way. Trying to please your ex adds to the stress and guilt they already have and adds to the energy you are putting elsewhere, and less for the path that is your own. That energy steals from your new life.

The deepest level of surrender is when we can let go of the emotional ties we have to our former relationship and partner. In this stage, we can completely separate ourselves from the relationship and the need to have our emotions tied to the other person. We are independent and understand there is a new meaning for the days ahead.

Finally, knowing the emotional intensity, bitterness, angriness, and regrets no longer exist are steps closer to surrendering. This can come when forgiveness is present and we understand there is a bigger picture for us. The meaning we attach to the breakup is huge in this case. If we see the past as lessons that we are grateful for, a different meaning is generated than if we are occupying our thoughts and feelings with anger and hostility toward the other person.

Letting go might be a task where the lines are not clear. Everyone has their own pace. Some prefer to surrender quickly and not to think about it any longer. Other people move at a more gradual pace and remove reminders, like pictures, slowly, and set up an environment without the ex as a concern on any level.

If a relationship has developed over time, an interdependency is often built with the other person. The interdependency can grow to an unhealthy point if not careful. One of the terms that was introduced over the years is called Codependency. The top recognized book on the topic is called, *"Codependent No More"* by Melody Beattie. Her book helps to separate our need to be dependent on another person when it becomes unhealthy for us.

Melody has another book with the title, *The Language of Letting Go: Daily Meditations on Codependency.* She mentions, "If we are unhappy without a relationship, we'll probably be unhappy with one as well. A relationship doesn't begin our life; a relationship doesn't become our life. A relationship is a continuation of life." She goes on to say, "Recovery is not done apart from our relationships. Recovery is done by learning to own our power and to take care of ourselves in relationships." That is a lesson for the future.

Benefits of Surrender and Letting Go

1. Less stress and anxiety.

2. More accountability to self (self-sufficiency)

3. Relaxes the mind and allows intuition to come in.

4. Pulls the immediate pressure off of emotions.

5. Removes drama when it is not needed.

6. Opens you up to additional input and better solutions.

7. Allows life to come to you instead of you pushing for it.

Surrender and letting go is not about quitting or failing. It is about not having to expend the energy or emotion to control situations.

Surrender contains an element of relaxation which brings good chemicals from the brain, including endorphins and serotonin. Both serve as natural antidepressants.

"Don't stress about the things you can't control from your past. Your past was simply research and development and the fuel for the great life ahead of you. It's crucial that you focus only on the things you can change and how you can create a better life for yourself now."

— Dean Graziosi

Stress is Reduced by Surrendering

Stress adds the chemical, Cortisol to our body chemistry, which then elicits a negative physical response and shuts down mental capabilities. Dr. Judith Orloff authored a book about Surrender. The name of her book is *The Ecstasy of Surrender: 12 Surprising Ways Letting Go Can Empower Your Life*. Judith shares tips to surrender stress, increase your brain's neuroplasticity, and feel younger:

- Don't sweat the small stuff. Let the little concerns and annoyances go from your life

- Cultivate gratitude and positive thinking. Tune into everyday experiences and create an attitude of gratitude and appreciation

- Be playful. Have fun. Take time away from responsibilities and worries and just have a good time. Fun produces endorphins and adds years to our lives. Find a way to incorporate fun into your daily existence

- Embrace humor. Read jokes. Laugh with people. Recall funny moments from your life. Laughing will extend the longevity of your life

- Get a pet. Studies show the companionship from pets extends your life and reduces stress and blood pressure. It also increases memory, which is an added bonus

- Practice forgiveness. Having grudges leads to high blood pressure and can lead to strokes, kidney failure and a variety of other health conditions. Let go of anger, resentment, and thoughts of revenge

- Meditate. Regular meditation helps keep you less anxious, calmer, and keeps the brain more flexible. Research shows stress leads to prolonged longevity, and prevents aging at a cellular level

Surrendering can make a huge difference in the quality of our lives and the longevity of our lives. If we remain stressed and trying to control a situation, like a past relationship, it has the opposite effect and shoots the stress hormone cortisol, as mentioned a moment ago, into our bodies which will cause premature aging in addition to stress.

Letting go is a skill to build like any other skill. It helps sometimes to start with small surrenders. For example, removing the need to be right in a conversation. Build small surrenders and notice how much better you feel.

If you have ongoing communications with your ex, and those conversations are stressful and contain conflict, see how you feel when you surrender and walk away from it instead of engaging. Just pick things in your life that you can easily let go of, and build on those experiences. After letting it go, just get in tune with how much better you feel. I used to engage heavily in conflicts and I decided my energy and emotions were too fragile to continue this behavior. I started advising my ex-wife that I had an engagement to get to and left suddenly. This started to change the interactions to a more position experience when I stopped by to get the boys.

One way to determine what to surrender to is to simply ask yourself, do I have control over this issue or decision? If your answer is no, it is an item that you can't spend much time in emotionally or mentally without making your situation worse. Learn what you can control and what you can't control and place your energy and focus on only items that you feel you can have an impact on.

The ultimate goal is to open yourself to more empowering emotional freedom. We all want to be more confident, centered, certain, creative, decisive, purposeful, resourceful, independent, happy, at peace, self-sufficient, flexible, cheerful, alive, and adventurous. We want to feel good. All of these positive emotions come from a new focus.

I had read a passage that has stuck with me for years now, and it was based on the principle that quality of life was more about what we remove then what we add. It was from a blog post by Timothy Ferriss, author of the New York Times #1 bestselling book, *The 4-Hour Workweek*.

My quest has been to remove anything that does not bring good energy or that adds stress to my life. This has paid off in a huge way for me. Before the divorce I was carrying the weight of the world on my shoulders. I had to get the house ready to sell in the divorce. We had to pay to fix things in the house as part of the process of selling (like a hot water heater). I had to still work beyond full time. I had the kids who needed me. I was dealing with my own emotional trauma. There was just zero room for anymore drama or items in my schedule.

If I didn't surrender at the time I had, I am not sure that I could have preserved my sanity. There are only so many internal and external conflicts that a person can handle.

One focal point that really helps when considering releasing yourself emotionally from your ex is to remember that letting go is to benefit yourself, not the ex. It will remove stress between the two of you when you remove yourself from the situation, but is for you to be able to open more energy for your own life.

Your ex had their opportunity to release you already. Now is your turn to take back your life and dignity and release them from your life.

It is a huge decision, but a vital one. Just as we made the decision earlier that the relationship really is over, knowing you are no longer going to be emotionally attached to them is the final step to letting go. You are surrendering in order for something better to come into your life. The way many people describe it is, "When one door closes, another opens."

Releasing Your Attachment or Fear

In chapter 2, I provided an exercise from Dale Carnegie about getting rid of fears and worries. There are a lot of additional tools that can help with the same process. If you have fears or attachment issues to your ex and about surrendering or letting go, another process is available. A man name Hale Dwoskin is the creator of *The Sedona Method*. The entire book is tied to letting go of fears and negative emotions, and it is worth a read. The book is called, *The Sedona Method: Your Key to Lasting Happiness, Success, Peace, and Emotional Well-Being*. Hale shares a process to surrendering and letting go of fear. I will share the shortened version with you.

1. Make yourself comfortable and focus inwardly.

2. Begin bringing to mind something about which you feel afraid or anxious - you may want to start with something small in order to see exactly what it is that your fear is going to encounter.

3. Give yourself a moment to notice if there is a strong feeling of fear or just a hint of it at this moment

4. Simply observe and welcome it, no matter if it is big or small.

5. Ask - could I let go of wanting this to happen? You may think that you don't want it to happen but know this is a negotiation with your brain.

6. Focus again on the fear and answer the following questions:

    a. What is it that you're afraid will happen?

    b. What is it you do not want to have happened?

    c. Now, could you let go of wanting that to happen?

Once you've gotten over the shock of the fact that you somehow want a negative thing to happen, it is often very easy to let go of the fear in this way because it is truly not what you want consciously.

Hale goes on to say, "Fear can prevent us from doing what we'd like or need to do, because we construct elaborate 'what if's,' or expectations, around taking action. Fear also stops us from letting go of our 'problems,' since we can't predict what will happen when we drop our guard."

There is an inner critic inside each of us that will try to give labels like, "You are not good enough." "You don't deserve her anyway." "Nobody will love you in the future." "You made so many mistakes in the relationship." "You were not good enough for him." "You are not lovable." And each of these make us rationalize fighting harder to try and get our ex back. Resist the urge. The person who dumped you has their own range of emotions they are experiencing inside. Many of the same labels you may have given yourself they could be adopting too.

You may be thinking that you want to create a friendship with your ex now. It is not a good idea, at least at this time, to try to remain close to them. The person who was dumped often tries to keep a connection by becoming friends.

More commonly the aim of becoming friends with your ex expands into a problem and anger and unresolved emotion is triggered in the mix and this can play out in a negative way with your ex-partner. If they began dating somebody else and you are working to maintain a friendship with them, there is a good chance that something is going to explode. If for any reason you are still believing you will have a future with this person, it could be at zero possibility if you try the friend angle. It could end with neither of you wanting future communications.

Part of surrendering and releasing is also the attitude and skill of forgiving your old partner. Again, this is more for your emotional sanity then for something that they are receiving. If you are to work through the anger, pain, stress and bitterness, forgiveness would be the ultimate goal. You don't have to even forgive them in conversation or by writing to them. To hold forgiveness in your heart is enough. Just release the negative energy attached to that person.

I have found that it was useful for me to journal from the point of hate, despising her, anger, and hurt, and continue writing until all I felt was peace and love. When you journal your feelings, it is just allowing you to process the emotions involved and get to the other side where you feel nothing but good thoughts and feelings.

If you prefer, you can write a letter in the same format as the journal entry would be used. When you get to the end of that letter and you feel better, burn it. Make it a ceremony to release all of the negative you are experiencing and adopt all of the positive that is in store for your current and future realities. The same process is useful with regrets that you have experienced.

After mounds of reflection I determined after the fact that I was an extremely good partner and I just didn't express myself to my ex because she had her own filters and thoughts as her focuses. I now know that we both had tons of value to offer. I am appreciative now because of the person that I became due to being released from my marriage.

I looked at my divorce as a chance to learn resilience and how to take on a huge challenge and come out better than before on the other side. I was young when I met my ex-wife and I made choices a lot differently in the past compared to what I do now. The relationship was built at a different time in my life and I am grateful now that I am able to fully re-evaluate my life for my remaining time on this earth. I was able to see the end as a new beginning and chance to do it at a better level than ever before.

"If I want to feel supported, I must support myself."

— Gabrielle Bernstein

When it comes to relying on people to support you, remember that others will not be there 100 percent of the time. They have individual challenges, and people will gradually start lowering support levels. Now is a great time to release the need for constant outside support. This is an internal shift to self-sufficiency and self-reliance.

Just remember to rely on yourself to transform this challenge into a better path. Taking full responsibility and owning the situation are the only ways you will make the shift needed, so better to own this starting now.

Remember that everything we hold onto in life just adds to the weight of the baggage we carry. It is good to simplify and let go of anything that does not bring you joy and things that add to your stress. Gabrielle Bernstein stated, "I've come to learn that I cannot hold onto anything – especially the small stuff. Surrendering it all is crucial to happiness." The quote is from her inspirational book, *Miracles Now: 108 Life-Changing Tools for Less Stress, More Flow, and Finding Your True Purpose.* The more we try to hold onto things or people in life, the more they elude us.

In closing this chapter, just know that each step of this process is about what you are gaining and not what you are giving up. One of my common phrases I say is, "It is what it is." After we are released by a spouse or partner, it really "is what it is." At first, I blamed myself and thought of all the reasons I couldn't please her. After layers of frustration, anger, and hitting my head against the wall emotionally, I came to the point of just saying, "it is what it is." It is a form of surrender. I then started using the word, "Next!"

I am much less tolerant now of anything that crosses my values. My boundaries are protected now and I have learned to be crystal clear about them in relationships since my ex-wife. I live my life the way that is genuine to me, and I surrender the rest. I just don't need a lot of control now. I have my standards and if something does not align...

Next!

Key Takeaways, Tools, and Lessons

- The decision about the split has been made for you. This gives you a great reason to surrender

- Staying on track consistently is the most difficult part at this stage. Know that you will have brief times where old patterns and thoughts sneak in. Get refocused quickly

- There are only two choices: Pursue the person and make the situation worse for both of you or, the second choice is to surrender and free up your emotions and energy for your own life. Trust that life will be better than ever

- Limit your interactions with your ex-partner even if you have ties where that require you see them

- The meaning you attach to the breakup is instrumental. If you want to live in peace, let the past serve as lessons and be grateful with what you have learned

- The lines are not always clear. Some people can release the past relationship quickly. Others step away gradually. The quicker the better as long as you are healing simultaneously

- Happiness is not a result of a relationship, it is something you already have or do not have entering the relationship.

- Taking care of ourselves and managing our emotions is something we must create as a cornerstone focus if we expect to be happy and at peace in single life

- If you are having trouble letting go of the relationship, start with small surrenders. One example is removing the need to be right in a conversation or argument. Just notice how it feels to walk away

- Releasing yourself from the relationship emotionally is for you, not for the other person

- Surrendering opens up room for better in your life

- Watch negative self-labels that are in the form of criticism toward yourself. When you think about shortcomings, often trying to get the other person back becomes a focus. Remember that your ex has labels of his or her own that they are experiencing now

- Forgiveness is a key to you being able to move on without so much emotional baggage. You can just mentally forgive them if you do not want to write them a letter or speak to them. Just let go

- Journal your hate or anger toward the other person until you get to a place of peace and love. You can even write a letter and burn it at the end, like a celebration for being able to forgive the other person

Chapter 8

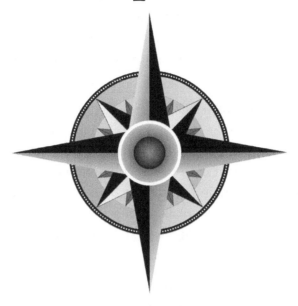

Thriving: A New Life
on Your Terms

"Your time is limited, so don't waste it living someone else's life. Don't be trapped by dogma - which is living with the results of other peoples' thinking. Don't let the noise of others' opinions drown out your own inner voice. And most important, have the courage to follow your heart and intuition."

— Steve Jobs

Steve Jobs touched on a very important point. A life of misery can result from living our lives based on the opinions and feelings of other people. Our time on earth is short. To reflect on how short, just look at how quickly the last five years have passed by. With only so much life to live, doesn't it make sense that we will spend it in a way that we are focused on a future built on our terms instead of what somebody else wants for us.

It is time to celebrate the progress we have made. This is new freedom to create life the way we want it to be. The ability to do this has always been present though maybe not applied. As Tony Robbins had mentioned, the past does not equal the future. The past is simply lessons for us to apply in our current lives that will lead to a more dynamic future based on our values. This moment will be gone as you read this sentence. Isn't it time to start treating ourselves in a loving and kind way?

We have discussed the importance of realizing that our past relationship is over, and surrendering so that we can align with something better. From here forward, the focus can be meaningful accomplishment. If we start focusing on what would make our lives magical, it is a lot easier to move on from the past.

One of the largest questions that should be answered by the time this book is finished, is, "What do I really want out of life?" I am not talking about what other people want for you, including the dreams of parents and friends, but what you really want the remainder of this lifetime to be. Later in this chapter we will spend time designing a future that will help you create a vision for what you want.

Setting Up the Rules to Win

One of the best focuses we can have is to set up our lives in a way that it is easy to succeed in our own minds. What I am talking about here is what we briefly touched on in a different chapter about how we have such huge expectations for ourselves but are not even sure where these expectations came from. When life doesn't match up to your perception of how the world should be, it makes it easy to feel like a failure and to be unhappy with life.

It is best to stay flexible about how you reach your outcomes from here forward. Knowing what you want to achieve is vital. The "how to" of reaching those objectives can be flexible. Just set up your life and objectives now to be in your favor, while being kind to yourself. This is another mental game we play. The ability to making it easy to win and hard to fail in our minds.

I know that people get sick of hearing how their mind is in control of their world. Still, without quality thinking results are bound to be more dismal. Richard Carlson, author of the book, *Easier Than You Think: Because Life Doesn't Have to Be So Hard*, states, "Our thoughts have the power, if left to their own devices, to take us to either great heights or miserable depths." The starting point of setting up standards for our lives is mastering this skill of using our thinking to our advantage.

Higher Standards Toward Our Outcomes

Our standards and expectations, especially when set up on hope and faith, can guide our direction effectively. This seems like it would be opposite of what was said in the last section, but it means to align with what is important and what you are not willing to give on.

Best-selling author, JJ Virgin, has had some huge challenges on her journey. Her story demonstrates the value of setting high standards for your situation. A few years back in 2012, a hit-and-run driver ran over her son and fled the scene. Her son Grant was left there to die. When emergency services arrived, grant was barely alive. He experienced severe head trauma and 13 broken bones.

JJ was advised by doctors that Grant would not live through the night. She was told to just let him go. The doctor stated that even if

Grant lived, he would lose his motor skills like walking, talking, or having cohesive conversations with other people.

JJ was not going to tolerate this diagnosis. She wanted the best possible chance of an effective recovery for Grant and to not only have him live, but to learn to thrive. Against advice from the initial hospital he was in, JJ had Grant airlifted to another hospital where she had optimistic doctors she knew who aligned with her philosophy of creating a better outcome for her son.

JJ had the same rounds of emotions that any parent would have when faced with the death of their child. She experienced negative emotions, hopeful emotions, questions and doubts about his well-being, but she never dropped her standard that she wanted for Grant. She refused to internalize what the original doctors gave as a diagnosis for Grant.

Grant did live, and his story is shared through a new book released by JJ Virgin titled, *The Miracle Mindset*. There was also a documentary done about JJ Virgin and Grant on PBS. The documentary is about the journey for JJ and Grant after the accident.

We get what we are willing to accept in life. We can set flexible rules and still hold a higher standard for ourselves. For most of us, it isn't as extreme as what JJ and Grant went through, but is our journey to do with it what we will. It is easy to get distracted at times of challenge. This is the time that we need to lift ourselves up and pushed through.

To achieve a life on our terms, it requires a realistic optimism. The goal of thriving is to go beyond just getting by. The commitment is required to create a life that actually holds bigger meaning. We are centered in a world that contains unlimited potential and power that we can tune into it any time. The outside world is always a reflection of the inside world of our minds. If we conquer our consciousness all else falls into place. Choice is always present.

We discussed how quantum physics shows the impact of energy in our worlds. When we vibrate at a higher level of energy we attract a higher level of result at the same time. When coming out of the breakup, energy is at a low level and often brings the disempowering emotions discussed in the early chapters.

To live a life where we thrive and make the most of our days, another commitment needs to include living with a higher energy vibration. In the book *The Power of full Engagement* by Jim Loehr and Tony Schwartz, the authors mentioned, "The more we take responsibility for the energy we bring to the world, the more empowered and productive we become." Thriving consists of energy management and thought management. Thriving also consists of having a clear picture of exactly what we want and why. Later in the chapter a complete goals process exists where you can the ideal future you want.

Quality and Life and Optimal Experience

We spoke about the importance of not just going through experiences, but *getting from* the experiences. Fulfillment is a larger success gage than just achievement of its own. Most people are very busy in life, but not doing things that matter or bring the emotional outcomes desired. There is a different level of living. The goal is to exist in an attractive state of mind whenever possible. As mentioned prior, the goal is to add more of what you want in your life and remove as much as you can of what you do not desire.

The ultimate goal we are looking for, whether taking productive action or destructive action, is to reach a more optimal state mentally. We want to change the way we *feel*. Our brains are always striving to get us out of pain and push us toward what we could consider pleasurable.

You may be thinking, I know junk food will not lead to pleasure for more than the few minutes is being eaten, but it is fulfilling a craving which is related to a mental state. Have you ever had something you did in the moment and knew it was not the best choice, but you were willing to get the long-term pain for the moment of pleasure it brought? The result we are always looking for is happiness. Later in the chapter we will review a framework of what can lay a foundation for happiness.

For decades Mihaly Csikszentmihalyi has been studying the psychology of optimal experiences. The premise is on people being highly engaged and focused on what they are doing, and an added sense of deep enjoyment of the activities the people are involved in. He calls it a state of concentration so focused that it amounts to absolute absorption in activity. When we are at that level of engagement, it makes it difficult to leave time for distractions, like the mucky emotions of a breakup.

"There are two main strategies we can adopt to improve the quality of life. The first is to try making external conditions match our goals. The second is to change how we experience external conditions to make them fit our goals better."

— Mihaly Csikszentmihalyi

Part of creating a life of meaning is getting clear what is important but in a way that simplicity is at the center. We can have a life full of goals and directions to take, but after determining the main outcomes we desire, the action or to do list is greatly shortened because not all to dos are needed to just achieve the result we are looking for.

Starting with outcomes we desire instead of just taking actions mindlessly (staying busy) is a huge mental shift. Most people will sit down and answer the internal mind question of "What do I need to do?" This question opens up a huge variety of activities that will be added to the list, whether an action may be needed or not. The mass actions will lead to a sense of overwhelm, and procrastination can be the result. The truth is that if you created a list of 30 items, only 10 might be needed to get the outcome you are going for.

Simplicity is the goal now so we don't give the brain mixed signals. According to Mihaly Csikszentmihalyi, in his book, *Flow: The Psychology of Optimal Experience*, "When we can imagine only a few opportunities and a few possibilities, it is relatively easy to achieve harmony. Desires are simple and results are clear. There is little room for conflict and no need to compromise." This falls in line with what is called Pareto's Principle.

Richard Koch, author of *the 80/20 Principle*, states, "20 percent of what we do leads to 80 percent of the results; but 80 percent of what we do leads to only 20 percent. We are wasting 80 percent of our efforts on low value outcomes. 20 percent of our time leads to 80 percent of what we value; 80 percent of our time disappears on things that have little value to us. 20 percent of our time leads to 80 percent of happiness; but 80 percent of time yields very little happiness." That is a mouthful, but at its core is that fewer activities in your life bring more of the outcomes.

Richard Koch's book, the *80/20 Principle* is based on the findings of *Pareto's Principle*, which was founded by an economist named Vilfredo Pareto. As Koch mentioned, Pareto stated the principle in similar terms. This principle specifies that 20 percent of the invested inputs (actions) will yield 80 percent of the results obtained. In other words, if we can narrow life in each category into only 20 percent of the actions needed to get 80 percent of our results, wouldn't it make sense to figure out what your 20 percent are? We touched on this discussion in earlier chapters but is one worth revisiting. It can be applied to situations and people in our lives. Again, some questions to ask are:

1. What are the 20 percent of thoughts and activities now costing me 80 percent of my frustrations and negative thoughts?

2. What are the 20 percent of the people who cause me the most pain and stress?

3. What are the 20 percent of the activities that give me the most joy currently?

4. What is the 20 percent of my current habits that are bringing results I want the most?

5. What are the 20 percent of my habits that are killing me in health, joy, and other positive results I want?

This principle can be applied to every area of life and can pull you out of overwhelm in a hurry. If all of life is based on our quality of thinking, this is a philosophy that is good to wrap your head around. Half the battle is slowing down a racing mind and thinking productively about what is next. Pareto's Principle can help you accomplish this, but does require sitting down and documenting what your most vital focuses and activities are.

Once you have narrowed to what is truly important in outcomes and actions, we can look forward to other elements that create a fulfilling life and help us arrive at a thriving state. The outcomes should be items that are very important to you. In each area of life there may be only a handful or less of important outcomes that make life worth living.

Keep in mind that just because we can connect to meaning and flow in one area of life doesn't mean it will spill over to other areas of life. This is why it is a good investment of time to decide, in priority order, what are the areas you want to achieve results in?

Even though Steve Jobs was heavily passionate about his career, near his death he expressed regrets about some other areas of life that were not related to career and wealth. Still, if he could do it all over again, would he do it differently? I am not so sure. We all have to learn to live with our decisions and regrets, but planning and action in advance could save heartache when we reach the later stages in life.

You may have noticed by this late in the book, the mind is the central tool that makes it possible to move beyond heartache and move toward the best of life.

Thriving and living a life on your terms is a mind game, no more and no less. Mihaly Csikszentmihalyi reminds us, "The good things in life do not come only through the senses. Some of the most exhilarating experiences we undergo are generated inside the mind, triggered by information that challenges our ability to think, rather than from the use of sensory skills." It is not possible to live at the highest levels of consciousness without the mind entering the equation.

Going forward, make the most of anything you *choose* to think about or take action on. The key is engagement and presence. Emotion creates life. If you are at work, make work as fun and challenging as possible. If you are with your friends, don't have your mind at work still. Wherever you are, be there. You will find that when you are engaged emotionally in whatever you are doing it will be hard to think about what is or what is not going well for you. The mind being engaged is the difference between time crawling or flying by. It is the difference between feeling drained or having huge reserves of energy.

There is one caveat that can make a difference. Make sure you take time to rest. Life can get out of hand if we get so present that the moments become years and quality experiences slip away. I was reading the story about Arianna Huffington, founder of the Huffington Post. She describes her story in detail in the book, *Thrive: The Third Metric to Redefining Success and Creating a Life of Well-Being, Wisdom, and Wonder.*

In 2007, Arianna arrived at what we could call an "aha" moment. She woke up with a puddle of blood from falling and hitting her face on her desk. When she fell in her office, she managed to break her cheekbone during the fall. She was working 18 days and was working every day of the week for a good portion of the time since starting the *Huffington Post* in 2005. After numerous medical tests done to determine if she had a condition that contributed to the fall, it turned out the culprit was simply mental exhaustion. It was a wakeup call for her.

With Arianna's life as what she describes as "completely out of control" she decided that it was time to redefine her definition of what success meant. Her current definition was not working for her. As she describes it, "In terms of traditional measures of success, which focus on money and power, I was very successful. But I was not living a successful life by any sane definition of success. I knew something had to radically change. I could not go on that way."

Arianna breaks her success definition into four key areas: Well-being, Wisdom, Wonder, and Giving.

After a relationship ending, it is easy to pick an area of choice to bury our time and energies into. Many people become workaholics, and others get into the pattern of getting home from work, opening a container of ice cream, and watching a marathon session of Grey's Anatomy on Netflix. Find time to balance a couple priorities and avoid the one-sided approaches and extremes like Arianna Huffington encountered. Her book is worth a read if you feel you are out of balance now. Quality of life starts with taking care of yourself.

The Anatomy of Happiness

Happiness seems like a far-off construct that is elusive and hard to keep in view for more than a few cherished moments. With mind entering the mix, we never seem to know when we are going to get knocked out of a peaceful and happy state of mind. The subconscious mind bubbles up some conditioned negative past memories that get us off track and suddenly happiness seems like it will never return.

I understand the elusive of happiness because I failed to have a framework in the past that could help me arrive back at positive emotions like happiness, peace, or passion. Knowing that my only choices were to feel good or feel like crap, I resolved to have more moments of feeling great and to leave unhappiness and its friends (hopelessness, fear, frustration and anger) at the door.

Happiness is not something we acquire. Happiness is something we tune into. We may have something that we really want and we think about it to the point we send signals of repelling energy toward the item. Happiness can elude us, especially when we take unhealthy actions that we feel will bring us this magical emotion.

I searched to see what I could find that were essential to happiness, so we can at least bring the central ingredients together to create an environment that can generate the state of happiness. There is no end all, be all of happiness, but the following ingredients seem to be involved when happiness is present.

Defining Happiness:

How do you currently define happiness? What makes you happy at the present moment? Are there situations where you have overwhelming joy and are alive with presence? When do you feel the most peace? Is there an environment like being outdoors or doing a certain activity? Are there moments that you can think of where you just felt peace and serenity and inspiration all flash in front of you because of what you were involved with? Define happiness for yourself and have an understanding of what it means to you.

The Absence of Ego:

It is natural for the ego to step in and pull us away from the unlimited and unfiltered internal part of ourselves. It can happen when we are in competition with other people, when we are worried about achieving significance in the eyes of other people, or when we start believing that our material things in life is who we are. Ego also forces judgment, even if the judgment is about ourselves. In an unlimited universe, there are no such concepts.

Dr. Wayne Dyer had mentioned that when we are in our mother's womb, we are not thinking about ourselves or whether or not we will be taken care of in this life. We simply exist. It is only after we are born and start getting conditioned by the outside world that suddenly labels and achievements become the cornerstone of our existence. When we just exist as we are, and not how we think we should be, happiness has a place to grow.

Living in the Moment:

There are many ways this condition can be described. Some call it presence. Others call it living for the moment. No matter how it is labeled, there is nothing we can do about the past, and the future is not here yet. This moment is all we have. We can have gratitude about the people, conditions and things we have, but also need to realize that being in the moment is where the power is. See Figure 8-1.

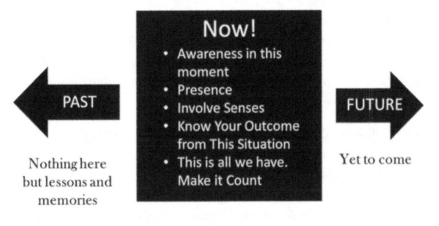

Figure 8-1

There is a practice known as mindfulness which can help us get more from each moment. In his book, *Wherever You Go, There You Are: Mindfulness Meditation in Everyday Life*, Jon Kabit-Zinn describes mindfulness as, "An ancient Buddhist practice which has profound relevance for our present-day lives. This relevance has nothing to do with Buddhism per se or with becoming a Buddhist, but it has everything to do with waking up and living in harmony with oneself and with the world." Jon goes on to say, "It has to do with examining who we are, with questioning our view of the world and our place in it, and with cultivating some appreciation for the fullness of each moment we are alive. Most of all, it has to do with being in touch."

Jon is one of the leading experts on Mindfulness and understands its value.

If we are not careful, we can spend years thinking about a past that has already happened with not a thing we can do about the results that have already come. We can be preoccupied with the future that is not even here yet, but the best use of time is to live in the present moment to create a future that lines up with our deepest motives and values.

If we are living in the past or in the future we lack awareness about what is going on around us. That awareness is what life is made of, and can bring meaning if we tune into it. When we understand what is crucially important to us in life, the present moment gives us the opportunity to take action, and practice those things which bring us the deepest sense of meaning.

Mindfulness does require us to practice focus and concentration. After a while it will give us better capacity for our mind staying secure and calm. Jon Kabit-Zinn says that we should concentrate solely on experience of our breath coming in and our breath going out or some other single object of attention. When we learn to focus intensively on the moment, we can develop a calmness that is difficult to disturb no matter what we encounter in life.

With today's world, it seems like focus and concentration are miles away. Yet, the most profound moments are those where we are in silence and can do what people describe as hearing ourselves think. When we are tuned into all of the outside noise in life it is like listening to an air conditioner run 24 hours a day, seven days a week, with a fan that is grinding. We require the chance to withdraw from the world and be awake to what is in the moment.

Most successful people in varying fields, have some form of a meditation practice. Culture often describes meditation to be like flowery or religious, but having some kind of mental separation from the world can be the most valuable time we invest in ourselves.

Many people consider meditation to be sitting in a fixed position praying out to the heavens. In mindfulness, it is more about discontinuing what you're doing and being present in this moment. It is more about being a witness to all that is happening now without trying to change anything about it. This would be a great place for self-dialogue about what you are hearing, seeing, and what may be happening around you. Just breathe and surrender and let things be right where they are. As Jon Kabat-Zinn says, "Give yourself permission to allow this moment to be exactly as it is, and allow yourself to be exactly as you are. Then, when you're ready, move in the direction your heart tells you to go, mindfully and with resolution."

Presence is a piece of mindfulness. I have a friend who taught me that it is good to know exactly what I want from every situation or interaction in life before I enter it. For example, when making a phone call or answering a text, what is your intention or outcome you wish to happen from the interaction? If it is simply answering or replying, a golden opportunity is missed to connect to another person.

Before my son comes over every other week, I ask myself what outcomes I would like to achieve when he is at my house. I design the week after these outcomes and ensure that he leaves with the emotions I wanted him to experience while he was at my house with me. In the days with my other son before he passed away, I lacked the level of connection I have with my younger son. I would ask him generic questions like, "How was school?" He would say "fine" and we would move on. I require a larger narrative and discussion with my younger son Devon. We talk about specific scenarios and people and I ask open ended questions that ensure I don't receive one-word answers.

So, what is presence? I turn to one of the most engaged and present people I know for the answer. His name is Brendon Burchard. Brendon is the author of the book, *The Charge: Activating the 10 Human Drives That Make You Feel Alive*. Brendon mentioned, "Presence means bringing your full attention and openness into now." He goes on to say, "Most people are so terribly busy and distracted that they never slow down to appreciate and take in the moment. And yet, in the present moment is where life is unfolding. And it is only here, right in the moment, that we can sense a oneness in connection with consciousness."

Back when I was utilizing alcohol in the evenings to numb the reality of my situation, I was anything but present. Before acquiring that habit, I was full of life and my energy was unstoppable. At the same time, my brain was on fire and I had to live off of systems to narrow my thinking level to where I was most productive. When I stopped drinking alcohol, I noticed my mind would race all day and all night. My sleeping was thrown off severely and I needed to be more engaged in my priorities instead of allowing it all to hit me at one time. It was a lesson about mental clarity and presence. When we experience a breakup, our minds are also very distracted. This is why the habit of presence is a necessity now.

I was reminded while reading Brendon's book, *The Charge*, that I was not very engaged with my life like I had been in the past. He had a question in the book that reminded me of times when my brain was sparked, and all I felt was purpose and inspiration. The goal is to live a more engaged, that is full of vibrancy and where we feel authentic. I knew that I would need to demand more of myself to get back to that place, especially after being crushed by a divorce I did not want and losing a son who had so much more life to live. The first step to getting back to an increased energy level was to shut out the past, plan the future, and live in the present moment. It has taken a great deal of conditioning to be back at that place. My goal now is to continue to build momentum toward being the best version of myself that I can be, which starts with the management of my emotions.

It was almost as if I was waiting for permission to take control of my life. Once I had shut down, it took a lot more effort to open back up and own the fact that I needed to create a life of substantial meaning and be bold enough to live it out. Even when considering writing a book that shares my deepest insecurities and experiences, I knew that the larger purpose was for others to build on my lessons and insights. Writing this book has required a level of presence and energy that I had not anticipated. I gave myself permission to move forward.

I challenge you to dig deep and create a standard to live by that will put life in alignment for you to your deepest values and the meaning you wish to create for the future. This means that you will need to adopt complete presence in designing a future that will charge you emotionally like we have been discussing.

Brendon Burchard offers one final thought that I feel can add value for you in this section. Brendon mentioned, "Everybody is looking for something, but he or she isn't sure what it is or where to look for it. The answers, as usual, are already within us. We simply have to understand ourselves better and activate the parts of us that make our lives rich, colorful, connected, and meaningful." In other words, we are back to increasing the quality of our thoughts to connect to meaning and emotion.

Letting Go of Rules and Expectations:

We discussed how our expectations often do not happen because of reliance on outside forces that can make things turn out differently than we expected. If we have strict rules for every area of life, and what it takes to be happy in that area, we are doomed to feel terrible when things don't happen the way we thought they should. Some of the magic in life comes from watching the way things turn out. We can start in a certain direction with the actions we take, but the outcome may turn out a little different than what we expected. Be open to what the universe gives you. You may find that it was the perfect fit for what you needed at that time.

The most insightful description that I can give you about having exact expectations and rules for each part a life is that these expectations are ideal and life doesn't always hand us ideal situations. If we go through life expecting that people will act in a certain way, most of the time, we are bound to be disappointed. Disappointment often leads to other negative emotions like frustration and anger.

The largest antidote is to have flexibility. You can have overall outcomes that you would like to see achieved, but be open to how they are achieved. Sometimes you may be surprised that something you did not perceive as ideal ended up being the best solution, after the fact. When we hold expectations, and do not allow for flexibility, disappointment gets in the way of happiness and peace.

Focusing on Failures as Shortcomings:

Perceived failures are really nothing more than learning opportunities that can be applied in the future. Perceived failures are nothing more than actions that turned out differently than we expected. This ties into the last quality I will mention about expectations. After an action does not turn out the way you want it to, learn what you can from that situation, move on, and don't use that approach again. In a relationship breakup, there are many lessons to be had if we look for them.

The largest lesson is to modify our philosophy or behaviors for future relationships, if it is indeed a shortfall on our part. Remember that sometimes the qualities and characteristics that you brought to your past relationship might be perfect for a different relationship in the future. Just because our ex had challenges with the way we handled something in the relationship, doesn't mean that it is something that we necessarily need to change with a different person for the future.

Being happy can be derived as a mental state much more effectively when we are not beating ourselves up over perceived failures. Expanding and trying something new is a much more effective way to tune into happiness. This leads to the next principle, which is personal growth.

Growth is Vital:

Expanding in a desired direction is a must. Throughout my life I have heard the term we are either growing or dying. I always thought that the statement seemed over dramatized. When I reflected more deeply about the meaning of that statement, I realized that it made more sense than initially pondered.

I used to travel a lot for work and I noticed that each time I traveled, I felt my senses kicking in and enjoyed the variety that came with different cities and different cultures. I felt that life was in motion and the energy generation increased dramatically. When I sit at home I feel stagnant and tend to settle into some negative habits and a more sedentary lifestyle. When I stopped traveling I had to figure out additional ways to grow my mind so that I did not feel neutral or declining in the way I was living.

One way that I get variety is to keep a reading goal in front of me so that I can constantly expand my mind. I get new ideas, and fresh ideas. From the comfort of my chair I feel that my solutions in life multiply as I read inspiring works. I am always striving to grow my skills and knowledge.

For you, growth can come in many forms and it is a matter of picking your preferences. Some people love documentaries, others are engaged by movies, and some even grow through contribution to their communities. The main point is to keep moving forward and create a momentum that does not allow us to sit still for too long and collect dust. Happiness is embedded in growing as a person.

Focusing on What is Working Versus What is Not Working:

Happiness tends to favor positive people. If we are consistently focused on what is going well in life, the universe tends to provide us more of what we are focused on. The same thing will happen when we are focused on what is not working in our lives. What is not working can be a starting point to discover more of what we can do to make it work, but that is the extent of what the negative focus is for. It is said that where attention goes energy flows. That is a beautiful way to sum up why we should be focused on what is working in life. That gives us a foundation to build on and more easily attract solutions, as mentioned.

Happiness breeds on solutions. When we focus on what is working, it is also putting us in alignment with gratitude. When we are grateful for what we have and what is working, smoother times seem to be the result. A state of happiness and peace is the goal, and when we are focused on solutions instead of problems, happiness grows.

Avoid Overthinking and Over-Analyzing:

Because of the level of distractions in life, and the massive amount of choices around us, it is easy to get in a loop of applying meaning to situations that do not require a meaning. There is no substitute for taking action and seeing how things work out, and then modifying our path.

I remember when I was stuck in fear and rejection, and all I did was run the same thoughts through my mind over and over again. I would try to guess when she was going to leave, and I gave false meaning to every possible situation attached to the breakup. I was miserable. When I reached the point that I said "screw it" I opened myself up to making solid decisions about where my future was going to go. It was a combination of being fed up and from having a lack of results to move my life forward. When I reflect on times when I was stuck the most in life, it was when I was giving labels to situations that ate up my energy and had me at the level of a victim.

When I made concrete decisions, devised the outcomes I wanted to achieve, and took the most direct and effective routes to get there, life moved forward and my confidence rose dramatically. It isn't easy to get out of your head when going through tough times, but when you realize that standing still is only making the situation worse, that is when over-thinking and over-analyzing can be avoided.

We are happiest when we are moving forward. There is nothing like lifting the weight off of our shoulders, which comes when we make unbreakable decisions and use simplicity to advance.

Happiness is a Choice:

Happiness is something that is chosen. It is an inside job. When we rely on external factors to make us happy, it is easy to fail. It is good to sit down and to evaluate what we allow to make us unhappy, and avoid getting ourselves into those situations. Thriving in life comes from reducing and eliminating as much suffering as we can. When we decide to be happy and not allow outside circumstances to impact that goal, we will see the existence of happiness and peace a lot more often.

Feeling Secure:

Before the mind can stop wandering and worrying, we must have the internal sense of security in our surroundings and minds. The brain will simply be too distracted to achieve a sense of happiness and peace until we feel we are secure enough. The trick is that a sense of security is in the eye of the beholder. One person can have $50 to their name and live in an alley with gunshots happening during the night and still feel secure. Another person could have a million dollars, live in residence with a doorman and security guard, and protected by key access and still not feel secure.

When I was in the Navy, I just realized that life came with risks and we cannot control when things can happen. I faced the reality that if I just lived my life and didn't worry about what could happen, I could relate to better experiences. Since the Navy, I also have the same philosophy when I get on a plane. Cars are tied to more fatality numbers than airplanes in absolute numbers, but people think negatively about flights because they are out of control once in the air. I just have the attitude now that if today is my day to depart this planet, then so be it. It allows me to stay in a more peaceful state. I am not saying that a person should not take precautions in their environment, but do not let your mind fill with doomsday thoughts based on something that is not fully in your control. Focus on living your life.

Last year I sat down to revise and notarize my Will, Living Trust, Medical Directive, Durable Medical Power of Attorney, and Durable Power of Attorney for Finance. My son had died and I had not taken the time to revise my legal documents, so I made the time.

I also cleaned out my entire home of anything that did not hold good energy or usefulness, and streamlined all I could. I donated tons of items to charity and friends in need. I condensed my basement to only a couple key boxes and a fireproof box for important paperwork like my birth certificate, DD214 from the Navy, insurance paperwork, deeds, car documents, and items my kids or executor would need in the case of my death.

People took notice of all of my streamlining efforts and I received numerous questions about whether or not I was dying. So, most people perceived my preparations to mean that I was dying. Actually, I feel more alive than ever knowing that I can live my life and know my love ones are taken care of. I am mentally ready for this universe to be in control of things I cannot control. More mental stress goes into trying to control outcomes that we have no control of. Leaving behind a streamlined process if I happen to pass away is a way for me to live in more peace now. It is one huge thing I do not need to worry about anymore. I can just connect with people around me and lessen the regrets I would have if I end up on my deathbed. Research shows that the largest item of mental anguish for people who are about to pass is the mounds of regrets they have remaining.

People search for security in a lot of ways. To some it is related to the size of a bank account. For others, it is through installing extensive home alarm system, purchasing a gun, or moving to a gated community.

Whatever you need to do to achieve a sense of security, find your way so your mind is at ease and you can focus on peace and serenity. Happiness grows when we feel at peace. It is my personal belief when we organize ourselves and set up for a life of our choosing, we are much better tuned into positive states of mind on an ongoing basis.

Sense of Belonging:

Obviously, we know the terms introvert and extrovert to describe whether we are a "people person" or more individualistic in our personalities. Whether we have a preference to living more internally or externally, it is still a human need to have connection. Some get it through meeting with family and friends, others log on and participate in blog conversations, and some join groups that meet with a joint passion or hobby. When we are involved with others who share a passion or interest with us, we are automatically more tied to happiness. The more distant we get from connection, the more our happiness can decline and isolation can build.

Happiness is a huge foundation for thriving and is something we should try to tune into as often as possible. Happiness is just one of many beautiful states of mind that can be accessed and adopted more consistently. If we set up the conditions for happiness, it will show up a lot more often for us.

Happiness is required to allow us to think our best and most productive thoughts. Instead of thinking happiness will just come if we do certain things, I believe that when happiness already exists, other desires for our lives come faster and with less effort.

Additional Tools for Happiness

In the book, *The 80/20 Principle: The Secret to Achieving More with Less*, Richard Koch outlines his Seven Shortcuts to a Happy Life:

1. Maximize your control.

2. Set attainable goals.

3. Be flexible.

4. Have a close relationship with a partner.

5. Have a few happy friends.

6. Have a few close professional alliances.

7. Evolve your ideal lifestyle.

In addition to the shortcuts above, Koch also offers habits that derive happiness. He states, "What we all need is a set of daily happiness habits, similar to (and in fact partially related to) our daily fitness and healthy eating regime." His seven daily happiness habits include:

1. Exercise.

2. Mental stimulation.

3. Spiritual/artistic stimulation/meditation.

4. Doing a good turn.

5. Taking a pleasure break with a friend.

6. Giving yourself a treat.

7. Congratulating yourself.

If any of these elements are attractive to you, include them in your plan. The point is to make sure you find a ritual that includes some of these, or all of these, in order to keep the focus on you and feeling good about where you are heading.

It is funny how everything we want in life, including peace and happiness, all are related to the quality of thinking that we have. In his materials surrounding emotional intelligence, psychologist Martin Seligman reminds us that "Moods like anxiety, sadness, and anger don't just ascend on you without your having any control over them... You can change the way you feel by what you think"

Happiness is by design, as is a future that is ideal for us. Again, remember that happiness and fulfillment is an inside job that we have control over, especially when we eliminate outside influences that we think will make us happy. Another instrumental part of a thriving life from here forward is passion!

Living the Passionate Life

"We'd all like to feel our life is purposeful. We all want to be passionate about what we're doing, to be excited about how we spend our days, to love our lives, and to feel were making some valuable contribution."

— Janet Bray Attwood and Chris Attwood

A thriving life begins with thriving emotions. There are little words more powerful than the word passion. Passion is used in the context of love, hate, interests in life, or just taking a stance on issues that are important to us. If we are living in mediocrity, have low energy and practically nonexistent positive emotions, then it can be difficult to know what to be passionate about.

The words passion and purpose seem to often be put hand-in-hand as an interchangeable term. Purpose is more our reason for being in a given situation, whereas passion is about the emotional intensity and frequency that we bring to situations. They do work together just as goals, the reason for achieving goals, and staying in line with our values all are a fit together. Because of this fit, we are loading all of the emotions and elements together to create a thriving life.

Passion can also be tied to joy. Psychologist, Joseph Campbell once stated, "When you follow your bliss doors will open where you would not have thought there would be doors; and where there wouldn't be a door for anyone else." Doors open when we are joyful and in tune with the joys and passions in life. We are in an open energy and this is contagious. Good things happen for us when our energy is right.

When we are in a rut, it is difficult to experience passion. I know I have had periods where I am working nonstop for weeks and I seem to feel dead emotionally during those time periods. The food started to taste the same, the days passed quickly and all blend together, and I felt like my verbal responses to people are even conditioned at that point. I have learned to take a step back from that and feel the joy of sitting outside with a book enjoying the sunlight. I draw passion from cooking different flavors of dishes at home. I get passion out of looking in my son's eyes and realizing he is the future, and passing on knowledge to him that lights him up. Passion can come from a lot of different places.

I'm sure you heard people say, make your passion your profession. But our core passions in life can be expressed through more than just a career. Janet and Chris Attwood wrote a must-read book called, *The Passion Test: The Effortless Path to Discovering Your Destiny.* To para-quote Janet and Chris, a passion does not have to be lived only through a certain line of work. A passion is more about how you are living your life. Janet and Chris described, "What you're after here are your passions, not your goals. Passions are how you live your life. Goals are the things you choose to create in your life."

In the way that Janet and Chris described passions, they are things that you love most, are most important to you and are most critical to your happiness and well-being. So, a question I thought of is, "What activities and topics in your life bring you the most joy? Janet had a conversation with best-selling author Jack Canfield, who is best known for his Chicken Soup for the Soul series.

In her book *The Passion Test*, Janet shared Jack's initial list of passions. So that you can visualize how a person would document their passions, I am including his list here:

- Being of service to massive numbers of people

- Having an international impact

- Enjoying celebrity status

- Being a part of a dynamic team

- Having a leadership role

- Helping people live their vision

- Speaking to large groups

- Having an impact through television

- Being a multimillionaire

- Having world-class quarters and support team

- Having lots of free time

- Studying with spiritual masters regularly

- Being a part of the spiritual leader's network

- Creating a core group of ongoing trainers who feel identified with my organization

- Having fun, fun, fun!

After Jack made the master list above, Janet was able to get Jack to narrow his list down to just five passions:

1. Helping people live their vision.

2. Being part of a dynamic team.

3. Being of service to massive numbers of people.

4. Having an international impact.

5. Creating a core group of ongoing trainers who feel identified with my organization.

Obviously, your list will be completely different. Jack's seemed to be more focused around career, but passions can be in each area of life. Janet mentioned some of her students and passions they had mentioned, some of which may tie into more of what you are looking for. Here are a few examples:

1. Having fun and everything I do.

2. Spending lots of quality time with my family.

3. Enjoying perfect health with lots of energy, stamina, and vitality.

4. Working with the supportive team of people who share my values.

5. Living in a beautiful home in which I feel completely at peace.

I suggest that you get a copy of your own of *The Passion Test* to walk through the entire passion test process because I will not be able in the short amount of space to do the process due diligence. She also frames the mind in a way that you can get the most out of the process. I will give some simple steps below, to get you started, but again it may be something you want to put more time into. Janet and Chris's book will be in the resource section at the end of this book.

Janet and Chris outline a few basic rules for taking your passion test. These rules include doing this as an individual process and not consulting with anyone else, doing the testing in one sitting, which should only take 20 to 30 minutes, if possible taking the test and a quiet environment without any distractions, and writing short, clear sentences and listing distinctly separate passions.

I will walk you through the steps of a passion test which will get you started, at least until you're able to dive into her book to put it all in perspective.

The Passion Test:

Step One:

Start with making a list of at least 10 of the most important things you can think of that would give you a life of joy, passion, and fulfillment. Begin each one with a verb related to being, doing, or having which completes the sentence, when my life is ideal, I am _____.

Step Two:

Compare the first passion on your list and the second, in which one you would choose over the other. Do this by moving down the entire list and then label your passions in order where you choose from number one forward if you keep number one and discard number two and then you compare number one to number three and choose and this will give you an order of value in priority of your passions.

Then if number three is most important to you, you would narrow to number three against number four, and so on. The goal is to narrow to your top five passions to ensure each is inserted into your reality. Just follow your first impulse as Janet and Chris recommend, and be honest and not worry about what others would choose for you.

Step Three:

Your list of your top five passions should exist now and you can give them an evaluation and rate them on a scale of 0 to 10. Zero means that you're not living in that passion in your life at all and 10 means that you are fully living it now. The intent is to get it down to five of your top passions so that you can live them any way and anyhow you choose. When you do the upcoming goal-setting process you can design your goals and future around these five passions.

Goals should be set up around creating an ideal life, not a possibility driven life. It is about designing a future that you will thrive on for the years to come. After effectively setting up an ideal future, it will seem like the breakup of yesterday is so far behind you, and you don't have much time to invest in even thinking about it because you will be so busy. Make sure that you invest all you have in keeping focused through the entire process of setting up your direction, which follows in the next section.

Thriving in Life Requires a Direction

We have done some basic action planning in Chapter 4 and creating some direction for activities that will please you going forward. These exercises were intended to help you get back on your feet when your state of mind state of mind was more negative was more negative, but we need an inspiring direction going forward.

According to Carmine Gallo, the author of *Innovation Secrets of Steve Jobs*, "Only 3 percent of people are committed to designing the life of their dreams." This statistic shows a lot of suffering around us. To get past the suffering we will need a working definition of what success means to us in life.

Many people think success means a huge amount of money, a Ferrari, the perfect relationship, a large house, never having to work again, or expecting very little problems on their journey. To other people success means having more peace and happiness than they do misery and internal conflict. It is all a mental game we play. Life will never be problem free and will never change until we change.

Our minds think in pictures and it is important to create pictures for the future we want. To show you just how important pictures are to our minds, I will give you an example of how this works. If I told you to ignore the yellow rabbit on the porch, could you do it? When I mentioned a yellow rabbit, did your mind generate a picture of a yellow rabbit on the porch? If so, you are showing normal reactions to the question.

I am attaching a full goal-setting process provided from Brian Tracy in his short but powerful book, *Bulls-Eye: The Power of Focus*. For any goal I set, I turned to Brian for the processes to make my goals real. He has a way of describing each step in creating questions to make it easier to form goals and plans.

Taking the time to create goals and a vision for yourself, to add to your purpose from here forward, is a monumental investment in your future. Reading is one thing, but sitting down with a fresh pad of paper to design a future and make it real is downright inspiring.

When you take on the following steps, have your favorite drink beside you, turn off your phone, clear any distractions in your environment, and put on some music that inspires the spirit of creation.

Set aside any thoughts or voices that tell you how you must think and what you must want when contemplating your future. The aim is to be 100% yourself and determine without filters how you want your life to be. Do not put limits on your thoughts. Keep the spirit of positive expectation inside you as you write.

Remember, if somebody else has done something that holds meaning to you, you can do the same. I read a book by Dr. Wayne Dyer where he mentioned that when he writes, he leaves his body at the door. In other words, he steps into mind and spirit when going into creation mode and lets nothing in the physical realm get in the way.

Before jumping into a process that will help you design the ideal future on your terms, take a few minutes to create a list of a new identity you want to create for yourself to head from now to the person you really want to be. Just write at the top of a sheet of paper in your notepad, "If I am being the ideal person I want to be, what qualities do I demonstrate on a consistent basis?" Some answers might be, unstoppable confidence, always know my direction, attractive personality, quick but effective decision maker, adventurer, saying yes to life, calm and cool on the inside and outside in my actions, results-driven, and any other qualities that are attractive to you.

Your identity is how you view yourself, and how others perceive you. Though your identity may be what others see, base this new "person" on who you want to be. Remember, the only opinions that matter are your own. Life is not only about what we *get*, it is about what we *give* and what we *become* as a person.

Now, let's dive into designing an ideal future that stands out as something that you really want for yourself. Get your critical mind out of the way. Once you have a pad of paper or spiral notebook and a pen or pencil ready, please follow the steps attached. Let the pen flow and try not to stop and edit as you go. Get out of your own way and you will have a working draft.

Step One: Make a Decision of Exactly What You Want.

Again, imagine that talent and ability are not a concern, you have all the skills and knowledge that you need, the relationships and contacts needed, and all the resources and financial support you need to achieve your goals. Set aside any past or present problems and limitations that you perceive yourself having. Be specific about what you want.

I am including some questions to get the thinking started. When answering, if you want to write down your items, you will be incorporating step two of the process. For now, write quickly and you can go back and add detail later.

- What ingredients are included in my ideal life?

- What do I want more than anything else?

- What could I devote 100 percent of myself to that will ensure the future I want?

- What is my legacy? What do I want to leave behind when I am gone?

- How do I want to be ideally physically?

- How do I want to eat? What does my physical action plan look like?

- If kids, how do I want my relationship to be with my kids?

- How do I want the relationship to be with other family members?

- How ideally do I want my friendships to be?

- How do I want my home to be decorated, room by room? How do I want the energy to be in my home?

- Where would I live if I had a choice of anywhere? What would my home to be like, ideally?

- How much money would I be earning per year if ideal?

- How much money in total assets do I want to have in 5, 10, 15, 20 years?

- Where would I like to travel?

- What skills and education would I like to acquire?

- What are the key values I want to live by?

- What kind of person would I like to become?

- What would I like to own that would supplement who I am as a person?

- What kind of future partner would I like in my life? (when ready)

- What adventures would I like to experience?

- What is my bucket list of activities I would like to do in a lifetime?

Step Two: Write Your Goals on Paper

Make sure that the goals you just set are written down on paper, or typed into the computer. By writing your goals down you activate the energy that will attract the resources, ideas, and people who can help you move toward your goals. It also gets your goals moving toward you from an energy stance.

Step Three: Set a deadline

Tell your mind exactly when you want to achieve your goal by. Our minds love to go to work on projects that have deadlines. Just go the side of each goal and assign a date to complete it by. You can pull your top one-year goals into one list and separate accordingly.

Step Four: List Everything You Need to Do to Achieve Your Goals

Write down everything you have to it do to achieve each major goal. This is the time to identify any skills or additional knowledge you may need to reach your goal. Also identify any obstacles that you may have to overcome. It is also good to identify people who can help you for each goal. When you write the steps down it makes a goal more achievable in your mind because it reinforces the belief that you can go after this.

Step Five: Organize Your List into a Plan

With the list you just created, organize the items into a plan. Simply organize your list by sequence and priority to keep from wasting precious energy. Identify the 20 percent of items on your list that will account for the 80 percent of the results that you accomplish. These should always be your focal points.

Step Six: Take Action on Your Plan.

Just get busy and do something to take you forward. This will create momentum toward your goals. Trust your prioritized list and take actions in order when possible.

Brian Tracy mentions, "When you take the first step on the path to your goal, three wonderful things happen simultaneously. First, you immediately get feedback that enables you to make course corrections, assuring that you were moving the fastest way possible toward your goal. Second, when you take the first step, you immediately get more ideas for additional actions that you can take to move ahead faster. Third, when you take the first step, your self-confidence increases immediately. You feel more positive and powerful. Your self-esteem and your self-respect go up. You feel stronger and more capable of achieving even more goals."

Step Seven: Take Action Each Day

Do something every day that moves you towards your most important goals. By taking actions toward these goals, you are developing momentum.

After completing the seven steps outlined, you have a plan in hand to thrive in the future and put the past behind you, permanently. The key is to always have something to look forward, with the focus on meaning. There are some additional philosophical insights that can make a difference in thriving.

Life Moving Forward

We are nearing the end of this journey together. My wish is that you were able to find at least a couple concepts and resources to grab onto that can improve the quality of the journey for you. A meaningful life is nothing more than stacking as many possible beautiful moments together as we can and reducing the amount of pain we suffer through.

There is nothing like this fresh start to build on with a life of passion, peace, meaning, and happiness. It all starts with curiosity and taking an interest in life. There are always new things to look forward to in life. Make the daily routine things that help you capture joy throughout each day. The joy isn't only in waiting for an event in six months. It is here and now. Obviously, it is good to have events to look forward. I once heard that if you live your life like you are on vacation you will not put so much time each year waiting for vacation to roll around.

The tradeoff between the grief that has entered your life and your ability to see something better simultaneously is key. You will experience moments where difficult thoughts occur. Just remember to turn back to all of the plans you have made for yourself.

Right now, it is important to make your voice the only voice. If it feels right to you, do not include the opinions of others. People have opinions and want to meddle in everyone else's life versus taking action to fix their own lives. Clean up your own life and then live it right. The future is bright and you need to be a part of it. There are plenty of actions you can take today that are good for you and fulfilling that can take the place of looking in the rear-view mirror.

I will leave you with a huge concept that can cause a quantum leap forward: **There are no rules. Your life is your life. You can make it whatever you want, and you can do it your way.** If you slow down and reflect on life you will notice that you know exactly what is right for you. That is your intuition and inspiration nudging you in the right direction. Follow *your* heart!

"Faith is trusting in advance what will
only make sense in reverse."

— Philip Yancy

Key Takeaways, Tools, and Lessons

- Life is short. Spend it on a way that is defined by your terms and not what others want from you. You have one chance. Don't spend it being miserable

- The past is no indication of the future. Stay focused on what is important today and the future will be the result of what happens today. Actions and decisions from 10 years ago have equaled the life you are living today. In 10 years your life will be your decisions and actions you are taking now

- Focus on meaningful accomplishment. If what you are doing is not holding meaning for you, switch quickly to something you decided was important to you

- Always be asking yourself, "What do I really want out of life?" The question will bring you back to a better direction when life gets difficult

- Set up to win in your life. Know what objectives are important for you in each area of life, but don't set up rules of how you have to achieve each objective. Sometimes you will arrive in places a different way than you expected. Love the journey

- Hold high expectations and standards for yourself without missing out on what is truly important to you

- Remember that optimal experiences are the focus. Keep a deep emotional engagement and concentration of the experiences you have designed in advance. Food tastes better, conversations are more fulfilling, and time flies as you enjoy your new life

- Remember that any behaviors you engage in, good and bad, are always intended to change the way you feel. Know alternatives that are good for you, and make you feel good

- Make sure that all you do contains meaning, but is centered in simplicity. Too many options will cause procrastination. Harmony comes through simplicity and narrowed options

- Live by Pareto's Principle in life. Narrow your actions to the 20 percent of the things that will bring you 80 percent of the results you seek. Also, narrow to the 20 percent of the people in life who support your cause and where you are going. Rid of the 80 percent that are doing nothing for your fulfillment

- Presence is everything. When you are relaxing, relax. When you are working, work. Get from each moment and have your mind on what you are doing. Use mindfulness to make your sensory experiences real time

- Happiness has a framework. Remember to: Live in the moment with mindfulness, let go of rules and expectations that constrict you, remember that failures are short-term and are lesson and not failures, and focus on what is working in life and drop the rest. Also remember happiness is a choice as is the feeling of security. Create a sense of belonging with people and activities that support your vision

- Determine and live your points of passion in life. Take the passion test and then find areas where you can implement your passions consistently

- Thriving requires a direction. Make sure to set up the ideal life on paper and make that your working focus from here forward

Lessons from My Divorce

"When faced with adversity, people often have two choices: give up or reinvent themselves and move on."

— Sam Schwartz

The 25 Lessons I Learned from My Divorce

Since I have encouraged you to build a toolbox that you can turn to during your recovery, I have brainstormed all of the ways to possibly help you. This chapter will summarize 25 lessons that came to me during the breakup/divorce process. Many were only discovered after excruciating suffering and emotional pain. If any jump out as applicable for you, write it down and include it in your own plan.

1. The sooner we can release our ex and get our focus off them, the more in control we become. Get off blame quickly and don't let it suck your energy and future.

2. The reason for a breakup is simply to serve us as a lesson for next time of what will and won't change in us for another person, what stays and what goes, what needs to be differently mentally, and what standards will become a way of life now.

3. Feeling miserable and depressed for prolonged times is a choice. We can apply the meaning to any situation. The time spent in dark places is a choice we make, whether we are ready to believe that or not. Deal with it quickly. Each moment eats up a part of life.

4. The consistent question to ask ourselves is, what's next?

5. Constant contact, stalking, saying I love you to the ex is just a way to keep us in pain, and reminds them of why they left.

6. The trick is to move away from denial and distraction quickly and assess where you have been so you can pull lessons forward and do it better next time.

7. The length of a relationship may be a badge of honor for you but staying together just because of time together is not a valid reason for keeping it alive. Don't perceive time together as a measurement of love.

8. You have such a perfect opportunity to build something now that is so much better than what you had.

9. Even if your values tell you to stay with one person forever, you are only 50 percent of the mix and sometimes have to face the fact that you can't think for the other person in the relationship.

10. Once I mentally stepped out of the relationship, I could see how dysfunctional I had become and how much I was neglecting my own feelings and values.

11. Once I re-scripted my life, there was no time or tolerance to feel sorry for myself. I had a new life and a new mission.

12. Take time to evaluate what you did well in the past relationship and what you will discontinue for the future.

13. Just be OK with yourself. At peace, at understanding, at having patience. Learn to love yourself because you are all you ever really have. Learning to quickly accept yourself and refraining from labeling yourself – especially off labels your ex gave you. Just because it was said does not make it accurate.

14. No matter what your new or existing living environment happens to be, make it 100 percent you. Make it ideal over time. Make it your tastes, your energy, and your preferences.

15. Be careful to always interject if your mind isn't look forward. Stay away from people who are negative or make you feel bad, or trigger bad feelings in you.

16. Stay away from friends and family who are not coming across as supportive. You will know because of the energy you feel around them. You may have obligation to be around some, but try to minimize that.

17. Read, listen to audios, and have constant exposure to resources that will help you gain new perspectives. Get out of the box!

18. Once you start working on the new life you have designed, you will be too purposeful and passionate to reflect too often on the old life.

19. Lay out your boundaries and standards of what you will and will not accept any longer. Make sure that others are clear about the definitions of how they can and cannot treat you.

20. Try to be as present as possible. Just flow with life. Sometimes the smell of fresh brewed coffee or hot tea is enough to spark positive emotions in you. Hear the kids laugh, feel the whirlpool after the workout, smell the healthy food cooking on the stove, and take in the air and breathe.

21. Have a place to retreat to in your mind. There is a place of peace and a place where calm memories exist and you can turn to at will.

22. Step away from conflict. Not just with your ex, but with anyone who is projecting their will onto you. Back up and give yourself space.

23. Be OK with your singlehood. Enjoy the freedom. Know that the night is yours to do what you want to do. Enjoy the quiet. Enjoy the music. Put on a great movie and turn up the volume!

24. Quickly establish rituals and habits. Willpower is only so strong, so have enough will to establish patterns over a couple months and the habits will take over.

25. Life is as depressing or as magical as we make it. I tried to remember what made me feel magical as a child and apply some it to my current life.

Resource List

The following list is in alphabetical order by title of each program. The Bibliography follows and has all of the sources used in this book.

Reacting: Dealing with Negative Emotions

Books:

Awaken the Giant Within: How to Take Immediate Control of Your Mental, Emotional, Physical and Financial Destiny! By Anthony Robbins. Tony breaks change and mastery into a science that can be replicated. This book brought me tools to change my inner dialogue and helped me get focused on where I needed to go instead of living in the past and the feelings of failure from my broken relationship.

Flow: The Psychology of Optimal Experience: Steps Toward Enhancing the Quality of Life. By Mihaly Csikszentmihalyi. By concentrating on setting up a life in alignment with the psychology of optimal experience, it is more difficult to concentrate on what is not working. This book offers the ingredients to setting up an optimal life.

How to Stop Worrying and Start Living by Dale Carnegie. This book is written in simple terms and gives some straightforward tools to dealing with issues impacting peace of mind

How to Survive Change…you didn't ask for. Bounce Back, Find Calm in Chaos, and Reinvent Yourself. By M.J. Ryan. I was shocked at how thorough this book was about the topic of unwanted change. It is not focused on relationships but has a good summary of strategies to use in unwanted change.

Mindset: The New Psychology of Success: How We Can Learn to Fulfill Our Potential. By Carol Dweck. This book contains the study of the mindsets of many successful people. You can copy the strategies these people use to go after solutions that were only obstacles before.

NLP: The Essential Guide – Creating the Person You Want to By Tom Hoobyar, Tom Dotz, and Susan Sanders. This book summarizes Neuro Linguistic Programming into areas of life in which it can be applied. NLP is a tool that can save you valuable time in your life when making changes.

The Journey from Abandonment to Healing: Surviving Through and Recovering from The Five Stages that Accompany the Loss of Love. By Susan Anderson. This book goes into depth about the grieving process encountered through the loss of love. This book is not targeted at relationship breakups specifically, but many of the symptoms are the same as other losses we encounter.

The Sedona Method: Your Key to Lasting Happiness, Success, Peace, and Emotional Well-Being. By Hale Dwoskin. The Sedona Method book contains exercises for addressing and releasing negative emotions.

Audio Programs:

The New Psycho-Cybernetics: A Mind Technology for Living Your Life Without Limits. By Maxwell Maltz and Dan Kennedy. The largest source of value this program brings is the expansion of the self-image. We can only grow our lives as big as the vision we have for ourselves, which is controlled by the way we see ourselves in terms of the value we have. This audio program is available from www.nightingale.com

The Zero Point by Dr. Joe Vitale. This seven-disc (or download) audio program will explain how to enter a mind state of zero, where all things are possible and limitations do not exist. This audio program is also available from www.nightingale.com

Developing a New Philosophy and Habits

Books:

Excuses Begone: How to Change Lifelong, Self-Defeating Thinking Habits. By Dr. Wayne Dyer. Though the title seems humorous, Wayne Dyer offers some ways to conquer habits and excuses if life that are more about tuning into ourselves mentally versus just taking action.

The Art of Living. By Bob Proctor and Sandra Gallagher. The importance of using energy and life and living at no limits is the cornerstone of this book. It is a light read that will raise your level of awareness in life.

The Compound Effect: Jumpstart Your Income, Your Life, Your Success. By Darren Hardy. In the Compound Effect Darren shows the power of compounded thinking and actions in life, both in positive terms of doing the little things and in negative consequences of not doing them.

Audio Programs:

The Day That Turns Your Life Around: Remarkable Success Ideas that Can Change Your Life in an Instant. By Jim Rohn. Any one thing can trigger a life change in us. This program sets up the conditions and momentum needed to change it all in a moment in our minds. It is about making the decision that enough is enough and it is time to move on. This audio program is available from www.nightingale.com

The Biology of Empowerment: How to Program Yourself to Success at a Cellular Level. By Lee Pulos, Ph.D. The deepest level we can condition in our bodies without getting into the spiritual realm, is at a cellular level. Lee teaches how rapid and lasting change can be made by understanding and conditioning the cells in your body. This audio program is also available from www.nightingale.com

Taking Control of Life

Books:

Create Your Own Future: How to Master the 12 Critical Factors of Unlimited Success. By Brian Tracy. This book is an investment you have to have if you are having challenges taking control of life.

Get Smart!: How to Think and Act Like the Most Successful and Highest Paid People in Every Field. By Brian Tracy. Brian is very straightforward in his books and gives a variety of tools in a short time with taking control and time management tips. He also gives insight on tool of effectiveness and getting the most from our efforts.

The 7 Habits of Highly Effective People: Powerful Lessons in Personal Change. By Stephen R. Covey. This book has been a top bestseller for years internationally. He teaches us about the importance of living from inside to outside and the levers of personal success and character.

Surrender/Letting Go

Books:

The Ecstasy of Surrender: 12 Surprising Ways Letting Go Can Empower Your Life. By Judith Orloff. Judith Orloff is a doctor who has seen her share of medical breakdowns due to people becoming over-stressed and out of balance. Why I like about this book is that she strongly makes a case for surrendering on things we cannot control and uses her own life as an example and experiment to making this happen.

Audio Program:

The Secret of Letting Go: The Effortless Path to Inner Success. By Guy Finley. Whether you are trying to free yourself from limiting beliefs or old habits that are tying you to your ex, this audio series can give you an additional framework for making that happen. This audio program is available from www.nightingale.com

Thriving in Life

Books:

Bulls-Eye: The Power of Focus. By Brian Tracy.

Living Forward: A Proven Plan to Stop Drifting and Get the Life You Want. By Michael Hyatt and Daniel Harkavy. The focus in this book is about getting on with life and stepping forward, which resonates highly with me since breakups are all about getting back on our feet, quickly.

Quantum Success: The Astounding Science of Wealth and Happiness. By Sandra Anne Taylor. After realizing that the entire world is energy and when I started tuning into my personal level of energy, this book opened the floodgates of thinking about the universe and being part of a larger consciousness. This book will shift your paradigm of what is possible.

The Passion Test: The Effortless Path to Discovering Your Destiny. By Janet Bray Attwood and Chris Attwood. This book guides you through a process of determining your top passions in life and implementing them into your everyday experiences. Read this with a notebook and pen close because you will need them with the exercises involved.

Awaken the Giant Within: How to Take Immediate Control of Your Mental, Emotional, Physical and Financial Destiny! By Anthony Robbins. Tony has an excellent chapter on setting up a compelling future that can add to your life directional planning with some great insights. I get a great deal of value out of all of Tony's works.

Audio Programs:

The Maverick Mindset: The New Science of Exceptional Achievement. By John Eliot, Ph.D. John offers a different way of thinking that maximizes resources and changes the way we approach our futures. It is a model of efficiency while using a different approach to get ahead. This audio program is available from www.nightingale.com

If You Do Not Realistically Feel it is Over

Books and video course by Michele Weiner-Davis. I am including the materials I have used of hers, but see her website for more selections at www. http://divorcebusting.com/

Books:

The Divorce Remedy: The Proven 7-Step Program for Saving Your Marriage. This book is written for marriages (or relationships) where the people are on the brink of a breakup, or are already apart, and need extreme measures to save the relationship. Though my marriage did not work out, Michele was the one who put me on a path of independence and gave me the nudge I needed to feel confident again in myself, with or without my marriage working.

Divorce Busting: A Step-By-Step Approach to Making Your Marriage Loving. This was the earliest release of her two books listed. I found what I needed in The Divorce Remedy, but both books hold incredible value.

Video Course:

This is an in-depth course on her famous "Last Resort Technique." I read the technique in The Divorce Remedy but it has more depth in the video series. Here is the link to the overview of the program on you tube https://www.youtube.com/watch?v=2RujdMzAjbk. Go to the divorce busting website for more details at http://divorcebusting.com/

If you would like to get an idea of Michele's style of educating, type in the keywords: Michele Weiner-Davis Ted Talk. Her name will generate a multitude of videos to view.

Please see the Bibliography below for additional ideas to help you on your journey.

Bibliography

Anderson, Susan. The Journey from Abandonment to Healing: Surviving Through and Recovering from The Five Stages that Accompany the Loss of Love. New York: The Berkley Publishing Group, 2010.

Anthony, Robert. *The Ultimate Secrets of Total Self-Confidence.* New York: Berkely Books, 1979.

Attwood, Janet Bray and Attwood, Chris. *The Passion Test: The Effortless Path to Discovering Your Destiny.* New York: Hudson Street Press, 2007.

Barrett, Jayme. *Feng Shui Your Life.* New York: Sterling Ethos (Sterling Publishers)., 2012.

Beattie, Melody. *The Language of Letting Go: Daily Meditations on Codependency.* Hazelden Foundation, 1990.

Bernstein, Gabrielle. *Miracles Now: 108 Life-Changing Tools for Less Stress, More Flow, and Finding Your True Purpose.* Hay House, Inc., 2014.

Burchard, Brendon. *The Charge: Activating the 10 Human Drives That Make You Feel Alive.* New York: Free Press, 2012.

Carlson, Richard. *Easier Than You Think: Because Life Doesn't Have to Be So Hard. The Small Changes that Add Up to a World of Difference.* New York: MJF Books, 2005.

Carnegie, Dale. *How to Stop Worrying and Start Living.* New York: Simon & Schuster, Inc., 1984.

Csikszentmihalyi, Mihaly. *Flow: The Psychology of Optimal Experience: Steps Toward Enhancing the Quality of Life.* New York: Harper Perennial, 1990.

Covey, Stephen R. *Primary Greatness" The 12 Levers of Success.* New York: Simon & Schuster, 2015.

Dweck, Carol. *Mindset: The New Psychology of Success: How We Can Learn to Fulfill Our Potential.* New York: Ballantine Books, 2006.

Dwoskin, Hale. *The Sedona Method: Your Key to Lasting Happiness, Success, Peace, and Emotional Well-Being.* Sedona, AZ: Sedona Press, 2010.

Dyer, Wayne. *Excuses Begone: How to Change Lifelong, Self-Defeating Thinking Habits.* Hay House, Inc., 2009.

Erber, Ralph, and Erber-Wong, Maureen. *Intimate Relationships: Issues, Theories, and Research.* Needham Heights, MA: Allyn & Bacon, 2001.

Ferriss, Timothy. *The 4-Hour Workweek: Escape 9-5, Live Anywhere, and Join the New Rich.* New York: Crown Publishing Group, 2009.

Gallo, Carmine. *The Innovation Secrets of Steve Jobs.* New York: McGraw Hill, 2011.

Gregoire, Carolyn. *What Hawaii Can Teach the Rest of America About Living Better.* The Huffington Post. 8/4/2013

Haas, Michaela. *Bouncing Forward: Transforming Bad Breaks into Breakthroughs.* New York: Eliven, (2015).

Harris, Dan. *10% Happier: How I Tamed the Voice in My Head, Reduced Stress Without Losing My Edge, and Found Self-Help That Actually Works – A True Story.* New York: itBooks, 2014.

Hoenig, Christopher. *6 Essential Secrets for Thinking on a New Level: Making Decisions and Getting Results.* New York: MJF Books, 2000.

Hone, Lucy. *Resilient Grieving: Finding Strength and Embracing Life After a Loss that Changes Everything.* New York: The Experiment, LLC., 2017.

Hoobyar, Tom, Dotz, Tom, and Sanders, Susan. *NLP: The Essential Guide – Creating the Person You Want to Be.* New York: William Morrow, 2013.

Hyatt, Michael and Harkavy, Daniel. *Living Forward: A Proven Plan to Stop Drifting and Get the Life You Want.* Grand Rapids, MI: Baker Books, 2016.

Jain, Sanjay. *Optimal Living 360: Smart Decision-Making for a Balanced Life.* Austin, TX.: Greenleaf Book Group Press, 2014.

Kabat-Zinn, Jon. *Wherever You Go, There You Are: Mindfulness Meditation in Everyday Life.* New York: MJF Books, 1994.

Keller, Gary and Papasan, Jay. *The One Thing: The Surprisingly Simple Truth Behind Extraordinary Results.* Austin, Texas: Bard Press, 2012.

Kersey, Cynthia. *Unstoppable: 45 Powerful Stories of Perseverance and Triumph from People Just Like You.* Naperville, Il: Sourcebooks, Inc., 1998.

Koch, Richard. *The 80/20 Principle: The Secret to Achieving More with Less.* New York: Crown Business, 2008.

Kushner, Harold S., *Conquering Fear: Living Boldly in an Uncertain World.* New York: Alfred A. Knopf, 2009.

Lipton, Bruce. *The Biology of Belief: Unleashing the Power of Consciousness, Matter & Miracles.* Hay House, 2008.

Loehr, Jim, and Schwartz, Tony. *The Power of Full Engagement: Managing Energy, Not Time is the Key to High Performance and Personal Renewal.* New York: Free Press, 2003.

Maltz, Maxwell and Kennedy, Dan. *The New Psycho-Cybernetics: A Mind Technology for Living Your Life Without Limits.* Niles, IL: Nightingale-Conant, nd.

Nepo, Mark. *Seven Thousand Ways to Listen.: Staying Close to What is Sacred.* New York: Atria Paperback, 2012.

Orloff, Judith. The Ecstasy of Surrender: 12 Surprising Ways Letting Go Can Empower Your Life. New York: Crown Publishing Group, 2014.

Proctor, Bob and Gallagher, Sandra, *The Art of Living.* New York: Penguin/Random, 2015

Robbins, Anthony. *Awaken the Giant Within: How to Take Immediate Control of Your Mental, Emotional, Physical and Financial Destiny!* New York: Free Press, 1991.

Rubin, Gretchen. *Better Than Before: What I Learned About Making and*

Breaking Habits – To Sleep More, Quit Sugar, Procrastinate Less, and Generally Build a Happier Life. New York: Broadway Books, 2015.

Rufus, Anneli. *Stuck: Why We Can't (or won't) Move On.* New York: The Penguin Group, 2008.

Ryan, M.J., *How to Survive Change…You Didn't Ask For: Bounce Back, Find Calm in Chaos, and Reinvent Yourself* New York: MJF Books, Fine Communications, 2009.

Schwartz, David J. *The Magic of Thinking Big.* New York: Simon & Schuster, Inc., 1987.

Sommer, Bobbe and Maxwell Maltz Foundation. *Psycho-Cybernetics Revised Edition.* New York: MJF Books, 1993.

St. John, Noah. *The Book of Afformations: Discovering the Missing Piece to Abundant Health, Wealth, Love, and Happiness.* Carlsbad, CA: Hay House, 2013.

Stone-Zander, Rosamund. *Pathways to the Possible: Transforming Our Relationship with Ourselves, Each Other, and the World.* New York: Viking, 2016.

Taylor, Sandra Anne. *Quantum Success: The Astounding Science of Wealth and Happiness.* Printed in Canada: Hay House Inc., 2006.

Tolle, Eckhart. *The Power of Now: A Guide to Spiritual Enlightenment.* Novato, CA: New World Library, 1999.

Tracy, Brian. *Bulls-Eye: The Power of Focus.* Naperville, IL: SourceBooks, Inc., 2015.

Tracy, Brian. *Get Smart!: How to Think and Act Like the Most Successful and Highest Paid People in Every Field.* New York: Jeremy P. Tarcher/Penguin, 2016.

Tracy, Brian. *No Excuses: The Power of Self-Discipline – 21 Ways to Achieve Lasting Happiness and Success.* New York: Vanguard Press, 2010.

Virgin, J.J. *The Miracle Mindset: Show Up, Step Up. You Are Stronger Than You Think.* New York: Simon & Schuster, 2017.

Vitale, Joe. *Zero Limits: The Secret Hawaiian System for Wealth, Health, Peace, and More.* Hoboken, NJ: John Wiley & Company, 2007.

Weiner-Davis, Michele. *The Divorce Remedy: The Proven 7-Step Program for Saving Your Marriage.* New York: Simon & Schuster Paperbacks, 2001.

Wimberger, Lisa. *New Beliefs New Brain.: Free Yourself from Stress and Fear.* Saline, MI: Gunn Inc., 2012.

Winfrey, Oprah. *What I Know for Sure.* New York: Hearst Communications, 2014.

About the Author

Daryl Moore understands the emotional turmoil that comes after an intimate relationship ends. Daryl was with his ex-wife for over 26 years. He was told by his wife that she wanted a divorce. Prior to his divorce being finalized, the family home was destroyed by a fire. To add to the pain, Daryl lost his son Dylan in 2015 to suicide. Daryl hit what he considered rock bottom and had to overcome fears and the emotional hole that had been created. Realizing that he had to pick himself up and start over, Daryl learned and tested new strategies to turn life around.

Today Daryl has reinvented his direction and lives a life on his terms. He has the privilege of helping others move past the negative aspects of a breakup using both personal lessons and tools he has adopted over the years. Daryl has a Bachelor's of Science degree in practical psychology from Regis University, an MBA from Regis University, and a Master of Science degree in Change Management and Organizational Leadership from Colorado State University.

Daryl has created his life in Colorado with his two children, Deidre and Devon.

Visit Daryl at www.afterrelationship.com

Or join Daryl on Facebook at:
https://www.facebook.com/aftertherelationship/

Notes

Notes

Notes

Notes

Notes

Notes

Made in United States
North Haven, CT
23 February 2023

33069242R00127